D1017600

Slack Line Strategies
for Fly Fishing

Slack Line Strategies for Fly Fishing

John Judy

STACKPOLE
BOOKS

Published by
STACKPOLE BOOKS
5067 Ritter Road
Mechanicsburg, PA 17055

Printed in the United States of America

10 9 8 7 6 5 4 3 2 1

First edition

Photographs by Jim Schollmeyer
Line drawings by Richard Bunse

Library of Congress Cataloging-in-Publication Data

Judy, John.
    Slack line strategies / by John Judy.
        p.   cm.
    ISBN 0-8117-1549-3
    1. Fly casting.   2. Fly fishing.   I. Title.
    SH454.2.J83   1994
    799.1'2 – dc20   93-8315
                                                                          CIP

For my mother and father,
Ann and Nelson Judy

Contents

I would like to thank my friend and mentor David Hughes for his help in creating this book. David has been encouraging my writing for many years. His assistance in the early outlining of this book and his help in finding a publisher have been invaluable.

1

The Elements of Slack Line Presentation

The slack started creeping into my fly-fishing strategies almost from the beginning. I was a young man just learning the delights of a fly rod on the mountain stream near my home in Colorado – a fresh convert from the bait and lure fishing of my childhood.

I would strap my fly rod onto the side of my motorcycle, stick a spool of leader and a small box of flies in my pocket, and ride up the dusty Denver Water Board road. I waded wet.

Anywhere above the diversion dam was good; it was not too touristy up that high. The tiny creek held rainbows, brook trout, and on occasion, if I was really lucky, a native cutthroat.

This little stream did not often call for distance casting – in places I could almost reach across it with a 9-foot rod. It was sneak water: I would creep up on hands and knees and lay short casts into the pockets.

One of my favorite spots, once I learned the key to it, was a little plunge pool. The water dropped a foot or two over the center of a natural log sill dam. Below the drop, the creekbottom was scoured deeply; the bubbles from the plunge gave the center of the pool an odd deep-blue color. This pool was just a little bit deeper than the others and was a preferred lie. It always held a fish or two slightly larger than the stream's normal 8- to 9-inch average. I could see these fish rising, but for a long time I couldn't catch them.

The problem was that there were multiple currents. The water bubbling up out of the hole beneath the plunge created a slow, swirling upwelling. These currents would then gather into a shallow tailout that accelerated into the next riffle. It was too open for me to get right up to the pool without spooking the trout, so I couldn't reach the upwelling without laying the line on the faster tailwater. If I cast normally, the faster water would pull my fly the moment it touched down. I had to find a way to get the fly to hesitate for just a moment.

After much experimentation, I learned to compensate by casting a little beyond the target and then, just at the right moment, making a calculated pull back on the line. This pull would create just enough slack to let the fly dance undisturbed among the bubbles for two or three seconds. That's all it took. I was so proud – it was my favorite little cast.

Years later, in retrospect, I realized that I had reinvented the wheel. The tactic I had created is called a bounce cast. Even in those days it was well known. But I was still proud because I had figured it out by myself. Slack line strategies had begun to creep into my fishing.

Most of what fishermen know about slack line fishing they learn through experimentation, just as I did on that little stream in Colorado. Unfortunately, too much of what we learn is reinvention.

Slack casting is a very simple idea. It is a problem-solving approach to fly fishing on rivers and streams. In moving water, almost every cast is influenced in one way or another by the push and pull of the current. Out of necessity we learn to compensate for these motions with a variety of tactics. There are many tricks; I'm sure you know and use some of them already. Mending, or looping the line upstream, is one very basic skill that comes to mind, but there are many, many more. The conglomerate of these tactics is slack line casting. It has applications with dry flies, wet flies, nymphs, or streamers. Curiously, though, slack line is not what most of us envision as fly fishing.

For the beginner learning to cast, the hardest thing to do is to get the line to lie out straight. There's never any problem creating slack. I still remember how well I could pile the line at my toes, as well as my frustration at not being able to get it to lie out straight.

I suspect early frustrations have a great deal to do with why straight line distance – the ability to cast the most line the far-thest – has become such a premium skill. It's what everybody strives for.

I have been to a million club meetings, fishing fairs, con-claves, and expos. When the casting starts, it's always the same. A few guys start casting around. The more experienced offer a few pointers to the less experienced. Then somebody starts cranking up the distance. The rods get bigger and heavier, and the next thing you know it's a contest. The double hauls start, and everybody tries to see who can hit the trash can clear at the other end of the parking lot.

I've never been a big fan of these power contests. You could accuse me of being a poor sport: I'm not a power caster, and I never win the distance games. But there's more to it than that. I really don't think these power contests have a lot to do with most actual fly-fishing situations. For that matter, I don't think fly fishing is a contest, but that's another story.

If you analyze your own fishing, I'll wager most of your fish are caught at less than 60 feet and after you have done some kind of line manipulation to reduce drag. They are not caught on long, straight casts.

One of the key elements that separates fly fishing from all other fishing is the fly angler's ability to control not only the fly but also the body of the line. A fly line has a small amount of weight in it. After it has been cast to a target, and in some cases even before the fly has arrived, you can manipulate the line in various ways in order to gain total control of the entire fishing system.

This control of the entire system is the key to fly-fishing success. It is a different challenge – not like straight line distance. It asks you to develop a whole new set of skills, but these are skills that will help you catch more fish.

Without exception, the best fly fishermen I know – those who really catch the trout – are good slack line casters. This sentiment is repeated again and again in fishing literature.

In his book *Caddisflies*, Gary Lafontaine says, "Teachers of varying opinions have influenced my casting methods, but it has always been the advocates of slack line presentation who were most convincing because they could prove the effectiveness of their methods by catching trout."

In *The Mayfly, the Angler, and the Trout*, Fred Arbona says, "The angler might as well resign himself to the fact that the beautiful picture-perfect cast is not the one he needs; in fact it should immediately warn him that he is going to have drag. . . . Casts with slack are the most useful approach in the real world of fly fishing."

Despite the evidence supporting the value of slack line casting, it is still not a widely accepted approach to fly fishing. In writing this book on slack line strategies, I hope to bring attention to these techniques and to the value of slack line casting.

Becoming a good slack liner is not necessarily difficult. It's a little like the sport of fly fishing itself: It can be as easy or as complicated as you want to make it. A fly fisherman can become a streamside entomologist or he can fish with a #14 Adams. Either way he's going to catch some fish.

In the same way, there are some slack line techniques that are quite complex, very difficult to master with any consistency. But on the other hand, there are also techniques simple enough that you can master them in minutes.

In the summers I am a working guide. From time to time I'm faced with the challenge of taking rank beginners on the river, some of whom don't even know which end of the fly rod to point at the water. I'm expected to get them fish. If I approached this problem from a conventional teaching perspective, we'd be dead in the water before we started. There is not enough time in a day to teach casting and then fishing and then hope my pupil can catch a trout by nightfall.

Out of self-defense, most guides have learned to teach a quick and easy, slack line approach to fly fishing. We use a floating line, a 9-foot leader with a strike indicator, and a weighted nymph.

I tell my clients that there are three steps to this thing: First you anticipate the drift, in order to figure out what you're going to do. I have my client strip out about 30 feet of line, clamp it with his finger, and let it drag on the river below him. Then I tell him to look upriver where he wants that fly to go—look to a position quartering upstream.

The second step is to cast and create slack. I tell my client to drill the fly right at the target. No backcast, no nothing. He takes

Basic nymphing illustrates the fundamentals of every slack line cast. Step one: Anticipate the drift—determine what you think the current will do to the line and fly.

Step two: Cast to the target. Sometimes slack can be created during the cast.

At other times, a second movement is needed to create a slack pattern to counterbalance the push of the river.

Step three: Control tension – tread the fine line between slack and drag. Have enough slack to create a natural drift but keep enough tension to strike when a fish takes.

the fly and indicator right off the water. Then, immediately after the cast, I have him follow with a large upstream loop of the line. A giant megamend. I ask him to lift the whole line and leader, right down to the indicator, and put it up above the fly, thus creating slack.

The third step is to control the drift. I now tell my client to raise the rod tip as the indicator comes toward him and lower it again as the indicator passes and starts to go away. He follows the indicator down the river with the tip of the fly rod, leaving just enough slack in the line to give it a free float but keeping enough tension to be ready to react the moment that indicator dips or twitches.

It usually takes about five to ten minutes to get somebody up and fishing with this simplified approach to the fly rod. Surprisingly, it often takes more time to get an intermediate fisherman going. The intermediates always want to do more than is required. They insist on casting overhead and stripping line, but these things only detract from the method. For experienced people it's just too simple: Cast, mend, follow through – that's all it takes.

Once the fisherman is doing it right and bouncing the nymph on the bottom, I know it's just a matter of time. I've created a fishing machine. All I have to do from there on is get the right fly on the end of the line and get the guy positioned so that there is a trout in front of him. The rest will take care of itself.

The beauty of the thing is that my client is fishing in minutes. He isn't battling a lot of complicated technique; within a half hour he's engaged in the sport and is looking around enjoying the river.

Of course, not all the trout that get hooked are landed. But my client is fishing and he has a very reasonable chance of success. To me that's a great beginning.

I think basic nymphing, like this, is a good place for even advanced fishermen to step out into the world of slack line casting. It is the perfect building block from which to learn the fundamental skills of slack line control. The enemy of the fisherman is drag – pull on the line. Slack is the tool to counter it. Tension is the fine line of control between slack and drag. The three steps used in basic nymphing apply to every slack line cast you'll ever make.

Let's look at these steps in a little more detail.

ANTICIPATE THE DRIFT

Slack line casting is not a matter of random slack piled all over the river. If the fisherman wants to battle drag, he needs to have control of where both the fly and the line are going.

If you don't know how the river will affect your fly, there is no way to know what pattern of slack you should create. You have to decide in advance how the drift will come out in the end.

Sometimes anticipating the drift is fairly obvious. With the basic nymphing technique, for example, the weighted fly will sink to the bottom and bounce along the rocks. As it bounces, the resistance will make the fly travel down the river a little slower than the line up on the surface. In order to get a longer drift,

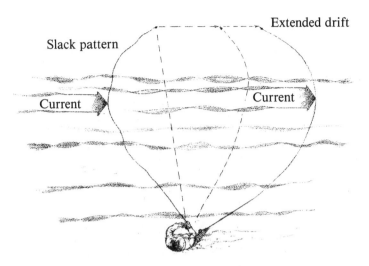

Extended drift

Slack pattern

Current

Current

A caster must anticipate the drift. In basic nymphing the fly, bumping the bottom, travels slower than the line on the surface; it also travels less distance. A slack pattern is created to counterbalance this difference by mending a belly in the line upstream. By creating this slack the drift will be extended.

you need to counteract this problem. You can anticipate the difference in speed between the line and the fly and from that develop a plan. Positioning the line above the fly will create slack. This slack will allow the faster-moving line to travel farther than the slower-moving nymph on the bottom, thus extending the period of time the drift remains drag-free.

In other, more complex, situations the effect of the current is not quite so easy to anticipate. But experience is a great teacher. With practice you get better at reading currents and guessing what they'll do to the fly. And in many cases, there is no way to understand the currents other than to practice with them. You try a cast, observe what happens, and then adjust and refine from there. In this way you should be getting better drifts with each cast.

It is quite surprising to me how many people do not bother to read the water but simply cast and fish by rote. They do the same thing over and over no matter what's happening to the fly.

On my trips on the Deschutes, there's a place at the bottom of an island where I like to stop on a gravel bar. There's a swift run there, which we approach by wading out into the slack water. Normally we fish it with the basic technique – cast, mend, and follow through. Then all of the line is out on the fast water. On occasion, however, a client doesn't wade out quite far enough. When he makes the upstream mend of the line, he may throw slack onto the still water just inside the fast current. Suddenly this is a very different drift. The line doesn't go down past the nymph anymore; it stays still, the fly swings almost immediately, and the fisherman gets no drift at all. All too often I see anglers who don't respond.

If I were in that situation, as soon as I saw that the line was trapped on the slow water, I would develop a new plan. I'd very quickly make a series of downstream mends to keep the line, which is now on the slower water, traveling at the same pace as the fly.

Moving an angler's position just a few feet can completely alter the way he needs to present the fly. In one situation on that gravel bar, it's all upstream mends; in another it's the exact opposite – all down. In both situations the goal is the same: to eliminate drag.

If the angler isn't watching and adjusting with every single cast, he'll miss what's going on and will spend all day throwing flies at nothing. As long as he fishes without making adjustments, he isn't getting the fly to the fish.

In slack line casting, nothing should be taken for granted. The good slack liner is constantly seeking ways to improve. He learns from his mistakes, always anticipating what will happen next and always seeking a better drift of the fly.

CAST AND CREATE SLACK

In basic nymphing, I ask beginners not to cast overhead, because a weighted fly and an indicator in the air can be trouble unless you are a reasonably accomplished caster. On more than one

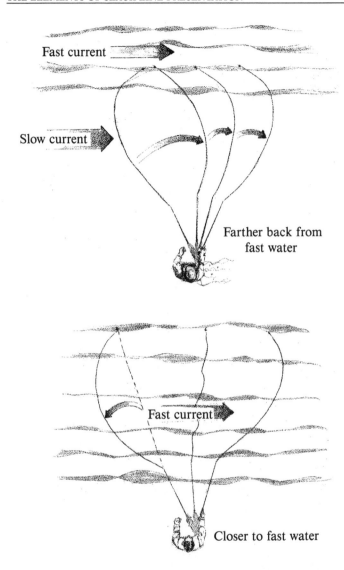

Fast current

Slow current

Farther back from
fast water

Fast current

Closer to fast water

Each cast is unique; the angler must continually adjust. Moving just a few feet can completely alter the drift and the angler's response. On a favorite gravel bar, standing in close means that the line lands on slower eddy water – the angler must mend downstream to counterbalance drag. Two steps forward and the line lands on the main current – the caster must mend up to achieve the same goal.

occasion, however, I have been criticized for this nontraditional approach.

"That's not fly fishing," some say. "That's nothing more than a bobber and worm. May as well fish a spinning rod."

Well, maybe so. But to me it's a stepping stone. I look at basic nymphing as just that—basic. It's a point from which to build upon.

I grant you that compared with the beauty and grace of traditional dry-fly fishing, basic nymphing is a bit crude. But on the other hand, an advanced nymph fisherman using the building blocks of basic nymphing and casting entirely off the water can be very skillful. Watching him fish is a thing of beauty—as graceful in its own right as the more traditional style of dry-fly fishing.

I feel that the slack liner should avoid becoming a traditionalist. That is not to say that he shouldn't seek to be an accomplished fisherman; basic casting skills are just as important to slack line as they are to any other side of the sport—in many ways, more important. What I mean by a traditionalist is someone who is locked into one way. Of greatest importance to the slack liner is that he not be unidimensional. He must be an explorer, a creator, and an innovator.

We all know that river currents are infinitely complex. Rivers behave in subtle ways. Different geology, different bottom strata, different currents make vastly different conditions. These different conditions make fishermen different, too. Every region and every river has its own style. There's an eastern style and a western one. There's a Montana style and an Oregon style, a California style and an Idaho style. And even within a state there are styles for the different rivers. In Oregon they fish one way on the Umpqua and another on the Deschutes.

Each of these styles has developed in response to the problems at hand, and the truly skilled angler is the one who can use as many styles as possible. Casting and fishing techniques are like arrows in a quiver. The more arrows you have, the more likely you are to hit your mark.

The fly fisherman who is serious about becoming a good slack liner should also become an artist who can paint with the rod. Throw off the narrow bonds of straight overhead casting and learn to use the rod in new and different ways. Develop a flexible casting technique that allows you to respond to the particular fishing situation. Each cast should be unique.

Learn to roll cast, to tension cast. Develop your curve casts and reaches. Improve the bounce cast and the mend. Each of these, at some time or place, will prove to be the tool you need. Be flexible so that you can respond to the river in new and creative ways.

CONTROL TENSION

The third step in slack line fishing is what differentiates random, useless slack from a controlled fishing technique. There is a fine line as to how much slack should be delivered in any given situation. There has to be enough slack to allow a free and undisturbed drift of the fly, but not so much slack that you won't be able to set the hook when a fish takes the fly.

How much slack is the right amount depends in many cases on how you are fishing the fly. With some of the swing tactics, like traditional greased line steelhead fishing or the Sylvester Nemes soft hackle approach, you are in close contact with the fly; you are fishing a relatively tight or "hard" line. You'll feel the fish immediately when it takes the fly.

At other times you may have to fish the fly way out on the "soft" side of control. There's a trout I call Harvey with whom I've had an ongoing relationship for years. Harvey is one of those wise, old fish that has chosen a resting spot that makes him almost entirely immune to fishing pressure. Harvey is so confident in his lie that he is actually a sucker. If I can get the fly to him, he eats it every time. But I only get one try. No mistakes. At the slightest sign of a disturbance, Harvey is out of there.

The cast is so challenging I can only get to Harvey, with control, about one time in twenty. I create piles and piles of slack that must be fed way back up under the bushes.

When I do it wrong and get too much slack, Harvey eats the fly, I pull back, and nothing happens.

Harvey looks at me as if to say, "Sucker!" and then *ptui!* – the fly comes bobbing back. I'm standing there on the bank with the fly line wrapped around my head and slack hung up all over the bushes.

Every once in a while I get it right. The slack comes out at just the right moment and I get control. Every time I do it Harvey is absolutely stunned. There is a moment of hesitation after I set the hook as if the fish were saying, "You can't do that to me!" Then all hell breaks loose.

My game with Harvey is the upper limit of slack control, pushing the bounds to see how far I can go. Newcomers to the slack line approach are often reluctant to test these bounds. They are constantly trying to feel the fly, to get contact with it in some way. This is especially true of fresh converts from bait and lure fishing methods.

And the slack looks sloppy. "I'll miss the fish with all those coils in the line," my clients complain.

The fact is that if you try to stay in touch with the fly, to use tactile rather than visual cues to detect the strikes, then the number of strikes is going to go way down. Slack makes the fly look natural, thus slack equals strikes.

I confess that with a slack line approach, there are days when my touch isn't right and there are fish all over the fly but I can't get a hook into any of them. When that happens, it's time to tighten up the control a little.

Anglers more commonly fish it too tight, however, and don't get there at all. I would urge you to experiment with more slack and explore the limits of control. There are times when the only way to get a drift is to pile on the slack. Don't be afraid to try it. You'll soon find out how much slack is too much; there is no way to know the limit until you've gone beyond it. Only through practice will you learn how to get control. Work at developing the skill of fishing "soft." The soft touch is at the heart of being a good slack liner.

2

Equipment
and the
River Currents

When I used to ride my motorcycle up the Denver Water Board road to fish, I was using an old Eagle Claw pack rod. It was like a portable broom handle with guides. You could pop the cork grip off, turn it around, and make the thing into a spin rod. Yet even with that club, I managed to start slack line casting.

I've always been something of a make-do guy. My career as a fish bum has left me with a somewhat limited equipment budget, and I've always found that compromise in equipment is effective. In order to fish slack, you don't have to have any special equipment. Whatever rod you currently own will work as long as it's reasonably well balanced. There are some advantages to certain types of equipment over others, however, and though it's not required, better equipment can make slack line presentation easier.

Currently in the fly-fishing world, there are two schools of thought on rod length. One group, largely centered in the East, tends to favor short, light rods. The special joy of this type of equipment is the feel. It's like a feather in your hand; you can cast all day and never get tired. With a really sweet rod, it's like pointing your finger, "Go there bug," and the line and fly respond.

The other group favors longer, heavier rods. The longer rods have more reach, which translates into better line control. If you have a 9-foot lever in your hand, you can do things that you can't with a 7½- or 8-foot one. With a longer rod you can keep line off the water, control slack, and mend better.

Clearly the slack liner wants these advantages. But on the down side, as soon as you start working with a longer lever arm, you are also gaining leverage the other way—back on yourself. A long rod feels heavy even if it is physically light in the number of ounces of graphite, guides, and cork. Its weight distribution makes it seem heavier. Weight distribution in a fly rod is much more critical than is commonly recognized. A very small amount of weight extended way out on the end of a rod will make it feel quite heavy.

You can get the idea by holding a broom in your hand. First hold it bristles down. The weight is fairly evenly centered in your hand, and the broom feels light and easy to wave around. But turn the broom around, bristles up, and it's heavier and harder to wave.

Somewhere a balance must be found. I started with an 8-foot rod, but soon I was discovering the joy of reach, so I replaced it with a 9-footer. That was so much better that within a few years I had a 9½-foot rod. I was really getting excited now. It was time to go for the ultimate: I started shopping for a 10-foot steelhead rod.

They didn't make very many 10-foot rods at that time. I should have known that there was a reason for this—conventional wisdom was saying, "This is not a good rod"—but I have to learn everything the hard way. This was going to be my ultimate slack line tool, and nobody could talk me out of it.

I refused to be discouraged by the fact that none of the shops had the 10-foot rod I wanted. I special ordered it. My pride and joy came untested, straight out of the catalogue.

What a mistake! My prized 10-footer was an arm breaker; I thought I was going to dislocate my shoulder with that stupid cannon. I found that I couldn't even use the reach advantage built into the rod because my arm became too sore to hold the rod up.

The only saving grace was that the rod gave me a good idea for a magazine article on rod balance. I suggested that if a rod is too long and feels too heavy, you can counterbalance it somewhat by using a heavier reel.

Upsizing your reel, even though it adds weight to the total system, draws the balance down toward the grip, making the rod feel lighter – like the broom, bristles down.

A rod in the 9- or 9½-foot range, counterbalanced with a heavier reel to improve the weight distribution, is just about ideal for slack line fishing. Shorter rods, 8½ feet on down, begin to sacrifice too much line control. I'd rather work a little harder and have the reach.

There have been definite improvements in the longer rods in recent years, and I keep hoping that advancing technology will find a way to make the superlong rods work, but it hasn't happened yet.

The second consideration when choosing a rod is line weight. Weight should be determined largely by the fishing conditions you favor: heavier rods for bigger streams and lighter rods for small ones. Don't go too light, however. These days it's a light-rod world. I often see people who are fishing undergunned simply because it's the trend. And I've been guilty of it myself.

I have a friend who double hauls a 3-weight all the time. "Why don't you use a bigger rod?" I ask.

"I like the delicacy of this one," he answers. But he continues to overwork the rod while nearby fishermen using slightly heavier rods fish more gracefully and effortlessly.

If you are going to fish nymphs much of the time, a slightly heavier rod can be an advantage. A couple of years ago during a three-day river trip, my favorite 5-weight nymphing rod was stepped on. The only thing I had for backup was a 7-weight, light steelhead rod. I'll be darned if that heavier rod didn't turn out to be a better casting tool! I'm still using it today.

When nymph fishing, you're often pulling heavily weighted flies up out of the water and handling leaders with big, wind-resistant indicators on them. The extra power of a heavier rod may prove very useful.

The worst thing about light rods is that they are fish killers. Again and again I see fishermen hook nice trout on undersized rods and then overwork and stress the fish because the rods aren't powerful enough to land the trout.

I take little delight in fighting a fish. It's a one-sided battle. I prefer to land the fish and end its stress quickly, then release it back to the wild. I take more pleasure in seeing a fish swim away healthy than in hearing the sound of a screaming Hardy reel engaged in an artificial fight.

When choosing a rod, especially a rod primarily for subsurface fishing, try one with a little more power. You may be pleasantly surprised with how well it performs.

The third characteristic in selecting a rod is flex pattern. You can measure a rod's flex fairly easily just by putting the tip against something and pushing until the rod bends. There are three general styles of rods on the market today: stiff butt rods, full flex rods, and progressive action rods.

The stiff butt rod, which on occasion features a fairly soft tip, tends to be a power and distance rod. To gain power, however, you'll sacrifice in other areas of performance. It usually takes more line to load a stiff butt rod properly, and the rod tends not to flex down into the handle very far. The stiffness dampens the feel of the rod to your hand. This rod handles best at distances beyond 30 feet.

The full flex rod, on the other hand, tends to be more sensitive. This rod has a very even flex from tip to butt and fishes shorter lines beautifully. On the negative side, however, the full flex rod tends to run out of power. When loaded heavily, it quickly reaches its optimum bend and simply runs out of gas, out of power, out of lift.

I fished for a number of years with a full flex 6-weight rod. I

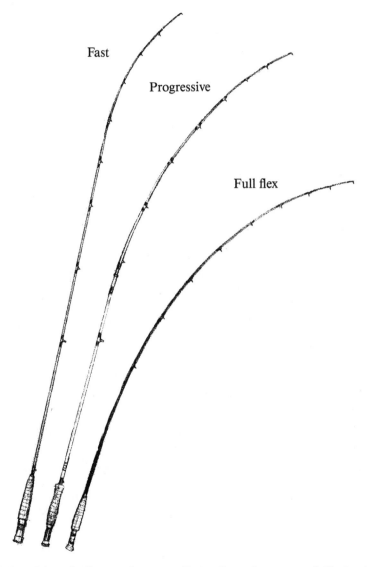

Fast

Progressive

Full flex

Flex of the rod affects performance. Fast action rods are powerful but not very sensitive. The progress action rod allows a compromise between power and sensitivity. Full flex rods are more sensitive, but lack power.

loved its sensitivity, but its lack of power frustrated me. Whenever I hooked a decent-sized fish, the rod would bottom out. It felt as if the rod handle were on a swivel. I could get a fish right up to me, but then I would chase it all over trying to land it. I couldn't fish nymphs with that rod either—it didn't have the lift.

A good compromise between full flex and stiff rods is the progressive action, or parabolic, rod. This rod tends to be soft in the tip, stiffening gradually through the butt. It has an uneven or parabolic bend when flexed.

The slack liner needs a rod that has plenty of sensitivity yet a full range of power. One minute he is using the rod to cast the full weight of the line and fly, possibly lifting a nymph and indicator out of the water, and the next minute he is using just the tip of the rod to mend and control small amounts of the line.

Because of its gradually stiffening taper, the progressive action rod is the best suited for handling this wide range of conditions. In light casting situations, only the soft tip section will come into play, allowing excellent control with only a minor sacrifice of sensitivity. At the same time, the gradually stiffening butt allows the rod to reach down into its soul and come up with just a little more power when it is being tested at the extreme end of loading capability.

The most important factor when you're selecting a rod is how it feels to you. Rods are very personal, and we all have our preferences. In the end, the best test is casting. After you've narrowed your rod selection to a handful of candidates, take the rods out and cast them several different times. Don't be afraid to pester the shop owners. If possible, fish with different rods—borrow them from friends. Sooner or later one rod will speak to you. That's the one you want.

Down the road the rod is going to become your friend. It will be like an extension of your arm—a living thing. So take your time and choose well.

Once you've selected a rod, you'll need to choose the right line or lines to go on it. The first question is which style of taper you want: double-taper (DT) or weight-forward (WF).

Literature produced by the line manufacturers says double-taper lines are better suited to roll casting, mending, and general handling of the line body. The weight-forward lines are distance or shooting lines. Since a slack liner is a line manipulator, he should favor the double-taper line.

In actual practice, the differences between these two lines are not that great. If the labels were peeled off the lines and they were handed to you to fish, you might have some difficulty telling which was which just by casting. The weight-forward *is* a better distance line and the double-taper favors control, but I learned to roll cast with a weight-forward line and I can also shoot distance pretty well with a double-taper.

I suggest that you not worry a great deal about the style of line you're using. Work toward the double-taper when time and your budget allow, but until then fish away with whatever you have.

More important for those fishermen who are working sub-surface is the choice between floating (F), sinking (S), and sink-tip (F/S) lines. Getting a fly deep, knowing it is deep, and keeping it deep is an ongoing problem for anyone who fishes subsurface in swift water.

My home river, the Metolius, is an unusually swift and clear body of water. It is intriguing to stare into the deep holes, sometimes 15 or 20 feet down, and wonder what might live down there. The swirling surface currents are disturbing, making it hard to see clearly, and the wild, native fish are beautifully camouflaged. But from time to time a clear window comes along in the currents, providing a good look at a fin, a tail, or a body moving off to one side. It's enough to provide the incentive for hours of fishing.

It was my attempt to get down into these holes and plunder the booty that started my white fly experiments. Somewhere along the line I got the notion to fish my nymphs with a large, white streamer tied on as a dropper above. The streamer allowed me to see where I was fishing and how the line and fly were behaving. It was like an underwater strike indicator. It was a marvelous experiment.

In the early stages of the white fly, my fishing technique was highly influenced by the writings of the late Charlie Brooks. The Brooks method uses a Hi speed Hi D full-sinking line and a large

weighted fly to penetrate the depths. The method was very effective and I caught plenty of trout with it, but it had its limitations.
In the Brooks method, the angler casts fairly straight upstream.
The fly sinks deep and comes back close to the angler's feet. But
there were times when I wanted to reach out, to fish toward the
center of the pools. As soon as I did, I started having trouble
getting the flies to go down properly.

My first reaction was to add more weight. I started tying
heavier and heavier flies.

Eventually I built a super colossus – little more than a salt-
water sinker with fur on it. Surprisingly, this minirock was only
marginally effective. It didn't sink nearly as quickly as I had
hoped it would. Despite its weight it seemed to settle like a
feather down into the deep water.

The weight experiment ended abruptly one afternoon when I
missed my cast, chucked, and forgot to duck. The fly hit me on
the back of the head. It sounded like a rock on a ripe pumpkin,
and I saw a great flash before my eyes. For a split second I
wavered above the river. I came within an inch of landing face
first in the water. I had a clear vision of what it would be like to
float unconscious through the rapids below. I thus learned how
much weight is too much to cast with a fly rod.

The next step in my white fly experiment was to explore
heavier and heavier sinking lines, from Hi speed Hi D, to deep
water express, to cannon ball line, and eventually to lead core.
This step didn't last long either. It ended when I watched a lead
core line and a white fly float down the river without sinking
more than 6 inches in a heavy current.

Finally the experiment took a turn in the right direction. I
began using line manipulation to sink the fly. I discovered the
slack line answer: current lanes.

In all rivers, various parts of the water move at different
speeds, forming parallel lanes down the river. An obvious example of a current lane would be a fast tongue of water pouring
down between two big boulders. In this situation there are clear
edges to the varying current speeds. Less obvious current lanes
appear on the surface of all moving water. On any river you care
to name, different areas of the surface will be moving at different

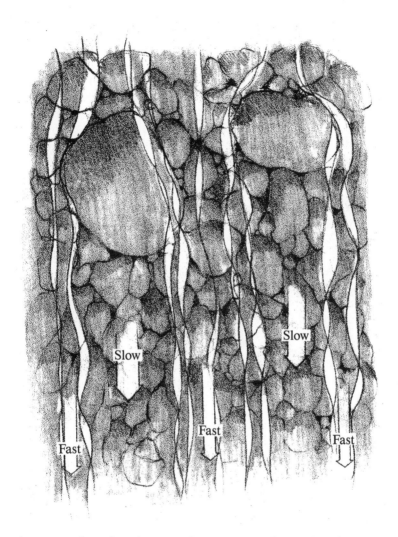

Across any piece of moving water there are current lanes. These lanes are created by bottom structure and affect the drift of your fly enormously. A line cast across the lanes will quickly start to drag.

speeds. There might be as many as half a dozen or more slightly different current speeds across a typical piece of flatwater. To get an idea of how these current lanes might look, spread your fingers wide apart; your fingers would represent the fast lanes, and the gaps between would be the slower currents.

Casting across these lanes has an enormous effect on your line and fly, whether you're trying to sink the fly or to fish it dry on the surface. The lanes set up a lateral push-pull on the line.

To better understand how current lanes affect your fishing, lay out a piece of string on the table. Push on it with one hand and pull on it with the other. An S curve will be formed in the string, while at the same time, the ends of the string will be drawn in toward the center.

We all know the shortest distance between two points is a straight line. If a force acts on this straight line from point A to point B, converting it to a curve, you would have to add line in order to continue to reach from A to B.

On the stream, if you cast across a series of current lanes, the faster lanes will push the line downstream, while the slower ones hold it back, thus creating S curves in the line. Since you're holding one end of the line firmly in place at the reel, all of the extra line drawn into the curves will be pulled from the far end of the line. Thus, as the S curves form, the tip of the fly line is being subtly moved toward you.

If the variations in speed of the current lanes are great enough, the pull on the end of the line may be quite significant — almost as if you were stripping in line. In a situation like this, your fly won't sink at all. This is how lead core line and a weighted fly wind up appearing to float downriver.

In more normal conditions, when the variations in current speeds are not quite so great, the effect of current lanes on your fishing is more subtle. This actually is even worse for the fisherman, because it is harder to discern what's happening. Here, the weighted fly doesn't float, but its sink rate will be significantly slowed. The dry fly doesn't look like it's dragging, but it is being moved enough to make it appear unnatural to the fish. The frustrated caster can't understand why the lead won't go down and why the fish don't like his fly.

The solution to the problem is fairly simple: Through line

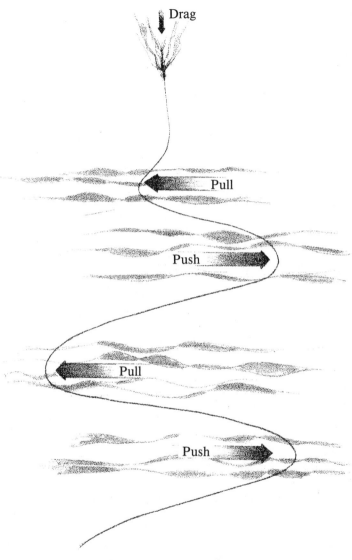

If a fly line is cast straight across the current lanes, those parts of the line on slow lanes will be held back; the portions on faster lanes will be pushed ahead. A series of curves will be forced into the line. The tip of the line will be drawn toward the caster in order to compensate for the extra distance in these curves, causing both drag and slower sink rates.

manipulation, the slack line caster must try to get the line, fly, and leader into a single current lane.

In the analogy of the lanes being like your fingers, if you lay the line across your fingers, it won't go through. Lay it parallel to your fingers, however, and it drops immediately to the floor.

When I was fishing the Brooks method with the Hi speed Hi D line, I was casting fairly straight upstream and the fly was sinking well because it was on one current lane. But the system failed when I cast out toward the center of the stream, because then I was involved with multiple current lanes.

Another example of placing the line and fly in a single current lane occurs in basic nymphing. Immediately after the cast, the angler mends the line and leader above the fly. This is done to extend the drift and also to improve the sink rate. When you mend you are placing everything—line, leader, fly, and indicator—in one current lane.

Sometimes when students are having difficulty understanding why I feel this mend is so important, I'll pull out the white fly to demonstrate the effect of being in a single lane. First I cast quartering up without the mend. Almost immediately there is a slight, imperceptible drag on the line and fly, and the white fly settles to the bottom very slowly. It usually is not in fishing position until it is opposite us, or even below. The length of effective drift is very small, only 5 or 6 feet.

Then I cast and mend the line, leader, and indicator above the fly. Now everything is in the same current lane. There is no pull whatsoever on the line or leader, and the fly plunges to the bottom in a matter of seconds. It takes no more than a couple of feet of drift to have the fly fishing effectively. It's on the bottom well before it reaches us, and the length of fishable drift is now 25 or 30 feet.

Yet another example of fishing a single current lane is casting a dry fly straight upstream. It's traditional to fish in this way because the technique is effective. It's effective because the line and fly are in a single current lane.

In most situations, the slack line fisherman is maneuvering the line on the surface to neutralize the effect of current lanes. If he wants to sink the fly, he fishes down through a specific current

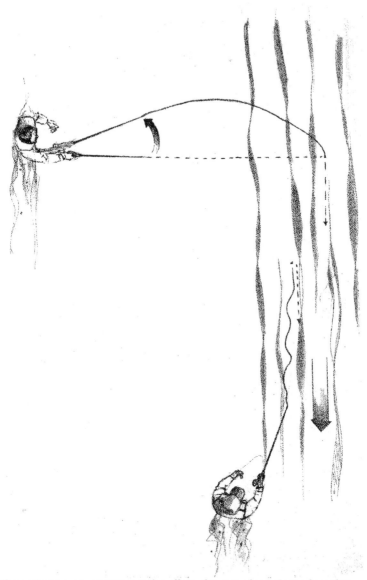

The easiest way to counteract the effect of current lanes is to place the line and fly on a single lane. Either mend the line so that the tip of the line and the fly are on a single lane or change position so that you are casting directly up or down the current lanes.

lane in order to get a drift. When he wants to fish a dry fly, he manipulates it in order to achieve a true dead-drift presentation.

I learned through my white fly experiments that in most situations I can get a fly to the bottom most effectively through line manipulation. I have almost entirely abandoned sinking lines and overly weighted flies. Even in the deep holes on the Metolius, I fish most effectively with a well-controlled floating line.

The best fly line for slack line manipulation is the double-taper floating line. Many clients call me before we go out on the river. "We'll need sinking lines to get down on the bottom, won't we?" they ask. "No," I tell them. "We can fish a sunken fly more effectively with a floating line. It's a matter of paying attention to the drift."

The single notable exception to the floating line rule is in certain types of steelhead and streamer fishing when you want to make an active (non-dead-drift) presentation by sweeping the fly across the bottom on a tight line.

The vertical presentation, typical of dead-drift floating line, delivers the fly down through a current lane. When the fly comes tight on the line at the end of the drift, it tends to swing up out of the lane very quickly. The tension comes from above and lifts the fly toward the surface.

The sinking line, on the other hand, will get both the fly and line down on the bottom. When the pull from the line comes, it's not from above but from the side. The fly then has less tendency to lift, and it will sweep across the bottom searching.

In any case, the sinking and sink-tip lines should generally be viewed as specialty lines; they should not be brought into use unless a specific presentation demands it. Ninety percent of your fishing, be it on the surface or underneath, can be done most effectively with a simple floating line and a good slack line presentation.

3

Simple Dry-Fly Situations

Not far below the boat launch there's a grassy bank that I like to fish. It's about 100 yards long, with an even current, not too swift, and a deep undercut. It's a very trouty spot.

I stopped in there with a friend and good client, Jack, who's a very solid fisherman – an excellent caster and quite knowledgeable.

It was a perfect morning. The summer caddis hatch was in full swing. The high bank was holding a cool shadow. The caddis were gathered dipping and bouncing, and the trout were lined up to feed.

"You want one of these soft leaders?" I asked, before we started. "I've been having some really good luck fishing with a longer tippet in conditions like this."

"Naw, I don't need that. I just put on a new leader," Jack replied.

"You sure?" I was trying to question Jack's decision without being pushy. "The soft leaders really fish nice."

"Naw, I don't need it," he said. So we started up the bank.

Jack is like a hundred – no, a thousand – other fishermen. We were faced with a classic upstream, dry-fly situation. It's the traditional way to fly-fish. Why would he want a special leader? Why would this be a slack line situation?

The answer is easy: microdrag, the subtle pull on a fly that, from a distance, a fisherman may not even recognize. Microdrag puts off more fish than most of us realize. Trout are incredibly sensitive to their environment. They are flight animals, and like all flight animals, deer, rabbits, and so on, they watch and they listen. Things that are not right in their world are vastly disturbing to them.

The fish feel the water – they know the currents and are particularly sensitive to movement. They can tell in an instant when something is not in tune with the river. A fly that doesn't follow every nuance of the current – even one that is only being pulled ever so slightly by nothing more than the stiffness of the leader – can put trout off.

Microdrag is very difficult for the angler to combat because it is hard for us to see. To us, a fly pulled by nothing more than the leader looks natural. We can't see what the trout don't like about it. But that doesn't matter; the trout sees what he doesn't like, and so we have to compensate.

This is why I strongly recommend the use of soft, or "spaghetti," leaders in any dry-fly situation.

I was first introduced to these leaders in the writings of Joe Humphreys, who credits his friend George Harvey with the origination of the idea.

The soft leader is built and tuned to collapse just slightly at the end of each cast. It is intended to lie out in a series of soft S curves, which serve to buffer the fly from any minor pull on the line or leader. Yet the leader still has sufficient control to make it easy to cast to a specific target.

The George Harvey soft leader is built from scratch by tying up small sections of various tippet materials to create a tapered leader. But I have found that these hand-built leaders can be fussy and take a lot of time. After some experimentation, I realized that most commercial leaders can be modified to be spaghetti leaders by adding a foot or two of tippet material to the end. I don't think there is any significant sacrifice in quality.

To build a spaghetti leader, I start with a good quality 9- or 10-foot commercial leader – the same leader I would normally use. The tip diameter varies according to fishing conditions. I trim off 1 to 1½ feet of the new leader, trying to nip it right where the taper first begins to thicken. Then I tie on about 3 feet of fresh tippet material, being sure to match the diameter of the leader and the new tippet. I do this, rather than just extending the tip, in order to keep an unbroken piece of tippet on the point. The leader is considerably stronger that way.

Once the leader is converted, it still has to be adjusted and fine-tuned. I watch its performance carefully. The idea is to get the leader to exhaust itself just as it finishes turning over. The leader should transmit just enough energy that it uncurls all the way, but not enough energy that it lies out straight. The perfect leader has just enough length to turn over and then settle on the water in soft curves. A leader that is a little too long will collapse and fold back on itself. The caster won't be able to control the fly and will have difficulty getting it to a specific target with control. On the other hand, a leader that is not quite long enough will continue to lie out too straight.

Adjustments to the leader should be made in small increments. A 3- or 4-inch change is often enough to balance the leader properly. It's surprising sometimes how fine the tuning is.

A second caution: Once you have a leader tuned, don't think it's over. You'll need to make further adjustments throughout the day. Little differences – a change in wind direction or a change of fly – can put the leader back out of tune. A soft leader has to be worked all the time. Keep an eye on your fly and leader to be sure they are performing properly.

If after a number of attempts you still can't get the leader to work, try another brand or style of tapered leader. I have found that oddly tapered commercial leader will simply refuse to be converted to a workable spaghetti leader.

With your spaghetti leader tuned up, you can get excellent

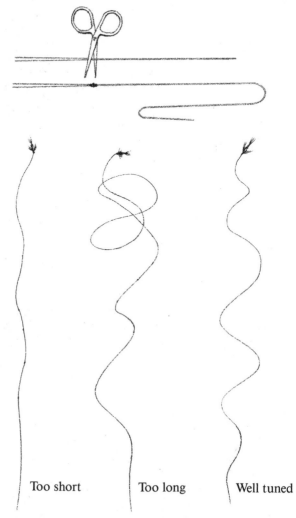

Too short   Too long   Well tuned

To convert a conventional leader to a spaghetti leader, cut the manu-
factured leader at the beginning of the taper. Knot back on a piece of
similar tippet material that is 6 to 12 inches longer than the original.
Fine-tune the leader by adjusting tippet length. A properly tuned leader
lands in small S curves. A leader that piles in a heap has no control and
must be shortened. One that lays out too straight has no slack; it should
be a little longer.

results. It's worth the small amount of effort and experimentation that goes into building one.

As Jack fished up the grass bank that morning, he put down the first five fish he came to. "What am I doing wrong?" he asked, turning toward me in frustration.

"I don't think it's you," I replied. "I think you need a softer leader." He had already checked the fly by catching a caddis out of the air and knew that he had a very good match.

"OK," Jack agreed, somewhat skeptically.

It took a minute or two to get his leader adjusted properly. I had Jack cast off to the side until we had the right S curves tuned in. "There you go," I said.

Jack cast back immediately to a fish that had just refused him. It came on the first cast in a classic head and tail rise.

Jack looked at me over his shoulder. "You're rotten!"

I shrugged and smirked. "I just wish all the fish behaved that well for me. I'd be the first rich guide in history."

A slack leader, however, is only as good as the cast behind it. To make the leader really perform, you must make the rod perform, too. A weak caster will find a soft leader a nightmare; it will be very difficult to control.

In chapter 1 I explained that I start beginners with a method that allows them to be a little sloppy in their casting. The basic nymphing approach to fly fishing covers a multitude of sins. But I like to make it clear early in the game that if a person wishes to progress beyond the basic stage, he must very quickly develop good fundamental casting skills. To become a dry-fly fisherman or an advanced nympher, and especially to become a good slack liner, you must have a solid foundation built around a good cast.

Casting has been taught by many experts; there are a number of excellent books and videos, and I don't want to rehash that work here. I can't move forward with the concepts of slack line, however, until a couple of building blocks are in place. The two key elements of casting that are particularly important to slack line strategies are loop control and a crisp rod snap.

The loop of the line is the "candy cane" that forms in the air when you are casting. An open loop is a big, fat candy cane like a round ball. A closed loop is a very tight, narrow candy cane in which there isn't much distance between the incoming and outgoing line.

Loop control – being able to dictate whether you cast an open or closed loop – is achieved primarily on the backcast by maintaining control of the rod tip.

Everybody – and I mean without exception every single person who ever picked up a fly rod – wants at first to dip the rod tip in the back. How many times have you seen a newcomer almost splatting the water on both sides? He's casting an open loop.

People do this because they equate casting with throwing – like pitching a baseball. In a typical throwing motion, you reach back on the windup to load up and get some energy into the throw. You go as far back as you can; the wrist even turns back to get an extra couple of inches.

It's this turn of the wrist that creates a problem in fly casting. As soon as you move your wrist with a fly rod in your hand, you move the rod tip quite significantly too. A very minor rotation of the wrist, just a couple of inches, has a dramatic effect when it is multiplied by the length of the rod. A movement of inches translates to several feet of arc out on the end of the rod. The most inadvertent flick of the wrist can rotate the rod tip from near vertical to almost horizontal. Most people do this without even realizing what is happening.

When the rod tip is rotated down in the back, it pulls the line down with it. We start casting with an arcing motion. The energy in the fly line is dissipated along the curve of the arc. There is no direction to the cast, and we end up creating the dreaded open loop.

The open loop is what causes all that slack beginners hate so much in those early grass-casting sessions. When there is little or no direction to the energy in the fly line, there is minimal power and the line comes out of the sky in a heap.

If a beginner makes the mistake of trying to cast a soft leader with an open loop, he'll find a new definition for frustration. He'll wind up with slack on slack and coils of line around his head and neck.

Do not think, however, that an open loop is always bad.

Wrist position controls the loop of the line. When your wrist is allowed to break back it dips the rod tip, creating an open loop.

An open loop, with a large distance between incoming and outgoing line, robs the cast of power and control.

There are times when, for a slack liner, an open loop might be useful and it is good to have a line settle softly out of the air. But it must not be accidental; it has to be your call. You have to learn to control your wrist in order to cast open and closed loops at will.

To create a tight loop requires self-discipline. The key is a firm wrist. By refusing to allow your wrist to rotate back, you keep the rod tip high and level and the line straight in the air. The energy in the fly line now has direction. There should be no dips or wavers whatever in the casting stroke — even the curves an advanced slack liner puts into the line are always created *after* the casting stroke has been delivered.

By keeping your wrist firm and not allowing it to rotate back even slightly, you force the rod tip to travel straight, the line follows, and the energy in the line is directed. You create a tight loop. With a tight loop you can cast with more control, big flies are less of a problem, and you can cast into the wind. The soft leader becomes a valuable tool.

The best way I know to get control over a floppy wrist habit is to look back and watch the loops form. Turn your head and watch your wrist and the fly line; you'll very quickly see your mistakes.

It is, however, almost as hard to turn your head while you're casting as it is to get control of your wrist. For some reason every fly fisherman's neck is welded forward, and it feels very awkward to look back. But I think the two things — wrist and neck — are interrelated; as long as you're learning self-discipline, you may as well gain control over both. Down the road, this skill of looking to control your backcast can pay big dividends in both tight loops and line control. Learning to look back puts you in control of what is happening behind you. You'll be able to analyze and aim your backcast. You take charge of the huge blind spot behind you. Learn to turn your head in order to control your wrist, and you'll soon have control of the loop.

There's a plant called a teasel, with a stiff, spiny, thistlelike head on a long, independent stalk. Teasels dry early in the season and then wait on the tops of high banks for unsuspecting fisher-

A firm wrist that is not allowed to break back keeps the rod at vertical, creating a closed loop.

A tight loop, with a narrow opening between incoming and outgoing line, creates both power and control.

men. Those fishermen with welded necks come to know the teasel well; they spend hours picking their flies and leaders out of these prickly things. But if you develop the ability to look back, you can direct your cast—make it a little higher when necessary, or take it a little to the left or right. You'll laugh at the teasels.

To determine whether you've achieved wrist control, false cast back and forth. Deliberately firm your wrist and cast a tight loop, then roll your wrist a little to form an open loop. Once you reach this level of control, your casting has taken a giant step forward.

The second area of concern in the casting stroke for the slack liner is developing a crisp rod snap at the moment of delivery.

My friend Rod Robinson, a casting instructor at Kaufmann's Fly Shop in Portland, Oregon, explains that "The casting stroke is a slow acceleration to a sudden stop." The slow acceleration Rod talks about is the loading or bending of the rod. As the rod starts

The casting stroke is sometimes described as a slow acceleration to a sudden stop. When the line has arrived at a straight back position the rod begins to move forward.

The slow acceleration loads the rod. Energy is stored as the rod is bent back by the pull of the line.

A sudden stop allows a clean release of the energy. The more complete the stop, the better the cast will be.

moving forward, it's pulling the line behind it. As you pull on the line, the rod bends back, like a bow ready to shoot an arrow. It becomes loaded with energy.

The sudden stop unloads the rod. It sends everything on its way forward. The rod's power is released in a quick burst of energy, and the line shoots on its way.

The problem most fly fishermen have with this part of the casting stroke is that they don't make the stop hard enough or crisp enough. They allow their wrists to roll through and their forearms to move. This loose link prevents the energy loaded in the rod from coming out in a single, clean release. It's a little like letting a bowstring go slowly and expecting the arrow to shoot out.

This problem goes back to the same old baseball-throwing mindset that screws up the backcast. A baseball pitch draws its power from the shoulder and upper arm muscles. The joints are loose. You snap the arm forward, and the shoulder, elbow, wrist, and even the fingers roll through to push the ball on its way. The energy here is in the looseness. Look at baseball cards and you'll see how those pitchers get their whole body into the throw for maximum power. They are so loose it's almost as if they were flexing their own arms, like fly rods, to produce the energy.

Most fly casters don't get quite that carried away with fishing, but we do use a toned-down version of the same motion when we are throwing the line.

If you pause to consider it, however, casting is not like the throwing motion at all. Casting is a motion to release energy from the rod. You can't throw a fly line like you would a baseball. It's a piece of string. How are you going to get it to go anywhere?

You can't.

What do we have to do in order to get the energy out of the rod and allow the rod to do its job? The answer is to make a sudden stop. Many casting instructors have addressed this subject. They all have their own way of trying to describe the feeling of making a sudden stop. Some call it a hammer blow, others say it's a push with your thumb/pull with your finger, and still others say you should drop your elbow or have a microsecond wrist. All of these descriptions are accurate. Every one of these casting instructors is trying to make the same point: stop suddenly.

Let's look at how this sudden stop works. In a typical casting situation, the bent rod has been loaded with energy. To get that energy out, you simply stop pulling on the rod – you stop moving forward.

The more abrupt the stop, the cleaner the release and the more energy the rod will send forward.

But it's not quite over yet. As the rod comes out of flex, any motion of the butt forward – any tendency for it to drift – will further dampen the throw and will soften the action. To get the rod to perform to its maximum, you have to stop cold. You should be like a machine – like a clamp holding the rod butt firmly.

Unfortunately, most of us, with the baseball mindset, stop the rod with a kind of rolling action. The elbow and wrist are not firmly locked but continue to come through the stroke in a follow-through motion. There is no crisp, clean stop defining the moment of delivery, and the cast is muddy.

To examine the correct muscle action, pick up a pencil, hold it in your hand like a fly rod, and then squeeze it as hard and as quickly as you can. Squeeze it violently. The muscle group that responds is the one you want to use in casting.

In an actual casting situation, you can try squeezing the rod grip to lock the forearm motion, but I don't recommend that you make this a habit, because it can create other casting problems. In final form, your grip should be loose, or at least not flexed tight, while your arm muscles stop the rod. After you've squeezed the rod grip a couple of times to help you understand the muscular action, you should be able to contract the right muscle groups without tightening your grip at all.

Good form will lock the wrist so it doesn't tip forward or back. The muscles on both sides of the forearm tighten sharply, and so do the biceps. The radius and the ulna – the two bones in your forearm – are stopped very abruptly in their forward motion by this muscular tightening.

The action is somewhat like throwing a Frisbee. In order to

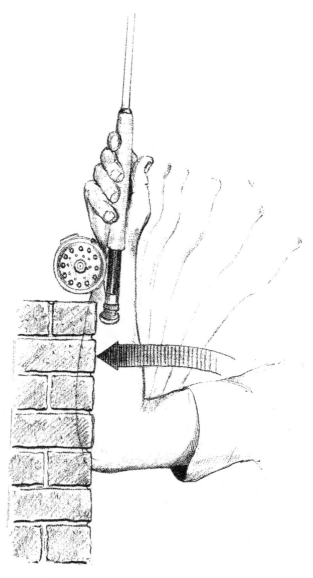

To create rod snap there must be a sudden firm stop of the rod butt. Tense the muscles in your forearm. Cause the bones in your arm to stop very abruptly, like hitting a wall. Keep the wrist joint firm; don't let it roll forward.

put a spin on the disc, you stop your arm motion to throw. You don't follow through with a rolling motion as with a baseball.

You'll know you've got the action right when your arm actually bounces back from the muscle lock. The stop is so sudden and so sure, it's as if your arm bounced off a wall. The recoil from the muscle tensing will make your arm bounce.

Learning this single skill – to get a good, crisp snap out of the rod – may do more to improve your ability as a fly caster and fly fisherman than any other single technique you will learn.

For me, good rod snap opened up new ways of thinking. It was a very important part of the genesis of this book. Things that happened to my casting and fishing after I developed a solid snap of the rod began to focus my thinking on slack line rather than on straight line tactics. I became much better at making the line and fly do the things I wanted them to do.

A natural offshoot of good rod snap is the bounce cast. When a soft leader is thrown with a tight loop, it comes down in nice S curves. Add rod snap to the mix, and the S curves can be amplified. They can be made to come all the way down the fly line to the caster. The technique is the same one I came up with years ago on the little stream in Colorado. Many fishermen use the bounce cast without even knowing it has a name.

The bounce is accomplished by aiming slightly above and beyond the target. The fly line is held tight. The cast is overpowered slightly – there's a little more rod snap than necessary. When the cast uncurls out at the target, it pulls against the rod tip. The rod flexes slightly and then bounces back. The line is pulled back and slack is added. The caster lowers the rod tip slightly to allow the slack to settle on the water in a nice, neat set of S curves.

By learning to control the power to the cast, a slack liner will develop a touch. He can make any pattern of S curves desired, from fine, little squiggles in the leader (a little tiny bounce) to a fairly large set of S curves down the entire line (a great big bounce).

The bounce has a thousand applications. It is one of the most heavily used tools in my casting arsenal. Virtually any cast made straight to the target can benefit from a little touch of the bounce.

One example of a good place for its use is Allingham Bridge. The pool at Allingham might be one of the most heavily fished 100 yards of water anywhere in America. This spot is between two campgrounds and on a road with good parking access. The trout there love to come to the surface. The fish will be rising at Allingham even if there is nothing going on in the rest of the river. The place is like a magnet to fishermen. It's a rare moment when there aren't at least two or three people there, even in the heart of winter. In the summer anything less than ten or fifteen fishermen is light traffic.

As testimony to catch-and-release management, despite the almost constant pressure there are still some very nice wild fish there, both rainbows and browns. But the wild fish at Allingham are not easy to catch. They have seen it all. They are the ultimate campground trout, and their finickiness is legendary. These fish

The bounce cast is created by overpowering the casting stroke slightly. The line bounces back toward the caster, creating a small amount of slack.

After the slack has been created in the air the caster lowers the rod tip to place the slack on the water.

The slack pattern created by the bounce cast is a small squiggle on the water.

have learned to hold out in the center of the pool underneath a complex set of currents. It's very difficult to get a clean drift without drag, and the fish inspect everything as if it were under a microscope.

When a newcomer arrives at Allingham, his usual tactic is longer and longer leaders, lighter and lighter tippets, smaller and smaller flies, and more and more frustration.

A better approach, used only occasionally by more experienced fishermen, is to tie on a good soft leader and use the bounce cast. The squiggles laid across the complex pushing and pulling currents allow slack to be absorbed so that the line does not pull the fly. Thus the microdrag is beaten.

The leader does not necessarily have to be extremely light and fine. Since I have become a slack line fisherman, I find that I have an increasing tendency toward heavier and heavier leaders. With good slack I have better control. I don't have to use an ultralight leader to attract fish.

I am becoming more and more like a fisherman I used to know years ago in Colorado, a man named Morris Long. Morris used to say, "Hell, if my leader isn't strong enough to pull out the bushes by the roots when I hook them on the backcast, then it isn't strong enough." I'm not quite to Morris's level yet, but I'm convinced that one reason for the popularity of the old "far off and fine" adage is that if you get far enough and fine enough, you've built a soft leader.

Sooner or later, if you keep extending out and reducing tippet size, the leader is going to start forming S curves and piling, and microdrag will be conquered. But control may suffer, too. You can't aim and you can't hook the trout as well with a long, sloppy leader, and when you do hook them they break off.

I prefer the slack line answer. Shorter, heavier leaders are easier to manage, they hold the bigger fish better, and they are not nearly as fragile. I spend less time fussing with the leader and more time fishing.

When I use the bounce cast and soft leader approach at Allingham, I can't say that every fish that sticks its snout up gets caught. No method is that good. But a fly fished with these slack line tools will bring a slow but steady round of rises. Enough fish will be fooled that I will catch one here and there.

Slack line is not a miracle cure; it doesn't fix everything in an instant. But a soft leader and a good bounce cast approach will create a steady improvement in your routine dry-fly fishing performance.

4

Downstream
Tactics

The British got us started on this business of fishing upstream
with a dry fly. On some of the famous chalk streams in England,
club members would not permit each other to cast to anything
except a sighted fish upstream. It was considered gauche to do it
any other way.

I'm not a Brit. I love my downstream tactics.

In Oregon, late spring to early summer is the season for large
stoneflies – the salmonfly and golden stone. Fishing these hatches
downstream with bushy, dry-fly imitations is about as good as fly
fishing gets.

It always surprises me that many fishermen don't know how
to fish downstream and don't think about fishing down even
when there are good opportunities. Upstream is strongly in-
grained in our thinking because it's been the tradition, but fishing
down allows us to get the fly to places we can't reach by any other

means. There are some very nice fish hiding downstream.

The various large stoneflies in Oregon crawl to the bank to emerge. Once out, they gather in swarms on the grass and bushes along the river. Stoneflies are notoriously clumsy crawlers. As they wander, swarming and mating, there is a steady drip of bugs from the bushes onto the river. The fish are lined up waiting. But they're not waiting in the wide open, out in the middle of the river. They're waiting where the bugs are, up under the bushes and trees.

There's an overhanging alder I like to fish during the salmonfly hatch. If I approach it from below, I always catch some fish. I can cast right up to the bushes, and if I sidearm, I can even cast under them a little.

But the biggest snouts always seem to be up in the hole. The largest fish like to hang out clear up under the bushes where the overhead cover is thickest. There they are protected from all but a few fishermen.

To get a fly into a place like that, I have to approach from above and cast quartering downstream, then feed out line and let the current carry the fly back into those deep, dark, cavernous shadows.

Downstream fishing begins with the bounce cast. When you cast upstream, the fly floats toward you, creating slack. When you fish down and away, the fly is taking slack, and you need to have a good reserve of line to feed out.

A powerful bounce cast is a good start, but by itself it usually is not enough. I add to the bounce by drawing back on the line after the rod snap to generate even more slack. The technique is called an S cast.

After the rod snap has been completed, you can manipulate the line with no adverse effect on the fly's travel on its way to the target. A fly will always go toward the spot where the rod tip was pointed at the moment of the rod snap. Manipulation of the rod or line after the rod snap will not affect the targeting of the fly.

Many beginners are apprehensive about moving the rod during the cast. They like to get the whole thing done—cast and let the line settle on the water—before moving the rod. There are, however, some very useful skills that call for manipulation of the line during the cast.

In downstream casting, I create the rod snap and then, while the line is still in the air, I pull back, drawing slack into the cast. It's important to have the slack off the reel and in your hand before you cast. As you draw back, feed that line in.

The amount of pull back and slack I add to the line depends on circumstances. Sometimes, in extreme cases, I'll pull all the way back until the rod tip is behind me in the backcast position. Other times it's less severe.

The pull back is not a fast motion. It's a slow, steady draw that acts to accentuate the bounce cast. During the bounce, the fly goes out toward the target and then comes back, creating slack. The pull back is an extra effort that creates even more slack.

As soon as the pull is completed, I drop the rod tip in the same way that I drop it after a bounce cast. The rod tip can come down suddenly to make a pile of slack for reserve, which can be very useful in some situations, or it can be lowered more slowly for greater control. It can even be wiggled back and forth as you drop it to make a very neat set of S curves, if you want to be tidy.

When I fish the overhanging tree during the salmonfly hatch, I bounce cast and pull back sharply, creating a very powerful S cast. The coils in the line let the fly sneak way back under the bushes. I usually get at least one nice fish, and often I can tease out four or five with this simple slack line technique.

Downstream fishing with the S cast and pull back is also very effective in slow, clear waters such as spring creeks, where the trout are superselective.

A couple friends of mine are Silver Creek fanatics. "With the downstream approach," they say, "the fly comes to the fish before the line or leader. We get a nice, clean drift without disturbance."

If the fish doesn't take on the first try—usually the case on Silver Creek—the caster can let the fly float right on by, then swing it off to the side, dry it so the spray goes away from the fish, and then re-present it without disturbance.

Casting upstream in the same situation, trying to curve the

The S cast is more powerful than the bounce cast. A larger slack pattern is created in the air.

A pull-back motion is added immediately after the cast to create even more slack.

The larger slack pattern is dropped onto the water by lowering the rod tip. A wiggle motion can be added to put an S curve in the line.

The slack pattern created by the more powerful S cast is larger than that created by the simple bounce.

line and leader around the fish in order to get a presentation, is much less effective. The caster will almost invariably splash the water slightly with the line or leader. After one or two casts, the fish are down.

I also like to use the S cast and pull back on the mountain streams in late June and early July during the golden stonefly hatch. The river I fish has a very even flow, and the plants and flowers grow right down to the water's edge. While the stoneflies are hatching, the flowers are blooming, too. It's such a pleasure to fish against the wildflower-covered banks that most people say it doesn't matter if they catch fish or not. But during the golden hatch, catching fish should not be a worry; some nice trout are active. Unfortunately, many of the tourist fishermen, who are not familiar with the river, start by wading up the banks to fish.

It's a very swift river. There is a fast strip of water out toward the middle, and a narrower, slower strip along the bank where the plants drag against the current. A classic upstream presentation is thrown directly across this current line. Because of the river's swiftness, even with a bounce cast the drift of an upstream cast is very short. The fly on the inside current travels much slower than the line on the faster outside current. The slack between the line and fly is quickly expended, and drag is almost immediate.

When I fish this river, I cast quartering down with a nice reserve of slack from the S cast and pull back. I am able to feed that slack to the faster-moving line in midstream. The tip of the line passes the slower-moving fly, almost seeming to pivot around it. Thus I get a much longer drift, and my fly is fishing effectively a much greater percentage of the time.

As I go along, I fish every inch of the riverbank. Sometimes it seems as if the fly is drifting in just a few inches of shallow water. But I don't hesitate; I fish it all. The banks are heavily undercut. The trout dart out from nowhere.

The native fish are as pretty as the flowers. They have a green-gold back and a bright crimson side stripe. The mature fish in the 15- and 16-inch range are little peacocks—the ultimate living rainbows.

The stonefly hatch on Oregon's lower-elevation rivers is

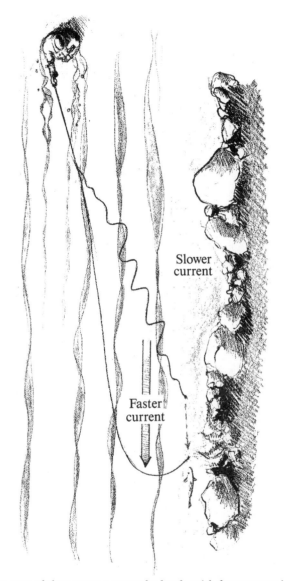

Slower current

Faster current

To fish an area of slow water next to the bank, with faster water in mid-river, face downstream and cast with a bounce or S cast to create slack. Use the slack to allow the line (in faster water) to pivot around the fly (on slower water next to the bank).

quite a different fishing situation from the mountain streams. For starters, the stonefly species is different – golden stoneflies in the mountains, salmonflies on the lower rivers. And it's also very different country. The mountain riverbanks are green and timbered, the water swift and tumbling. The lower-elevation streams are in the high desert, stark and beautiful, with towering canyon walls.

The mountain streams call for what I term hummingbird fishing: repeated casts and short drifts. The swift water prevents a long float. I try to cover 6 or 8 feet of the bank with each drift and then move on – cast and move; cast and move. By covering a lot of ground, I present to as many fish as possible.

On the lower streams there are more places where slow currents meander back up under the overhanging bushes. The caster needs long, extended drifts that find their way back into these grottoes.

My friend and neighbor Bob Newton is a master of the super-long downstream dry-fly presentation. I've watched Bob stand on a shallow flat and drift flies 60, 70, 80 feet down below him. His drifts are so long that when he's finished, he's holding on to the end of the fly line and the start of the backing. Every inch of that enormous drift is a perfect float.

Bob uses a technique of flipping the line after the initial S cast and pull back to generate additional slack: The original slack is used to create even more slack.

When he executes the flip, Bob makes a small upward or side-to-side casting motion with the tip of the rod. He holds the rod tip low, just over the water, and flips it. Surface tension helps to run the line out through the guides. The original slack created by the S cast and pull back buffers the fly from the flipping motion so it isn't jerked across the water.

Each flip will run out a couple of feet of slack. By stripping line off the reel and making repeated flips, Bob can nurse out a considerable amount of line. In the right conditions, there is almost no limit to how far a fly can be drifted.

One of my favorite spots in which to use Bob's technique is a sandbar at the back of a large eddy, accessible only by boat. I park on the sandbar and we cast in toward shore. Between the

To create slack with the flip method, have the line in your hand ready to feed out through the guides.

Flip the rod tip up and down or side to side to work line out through the guides. Take care to keep a small buffer of slack between you and the fly.

shore and the sandbar there is a small, slow-moving back channel. Except for a couple of gaps, this channel is almost entirely overhung with alders.

We cast as far back into the gaps as we can, trying to get the fly as close to the bank as possible. Then we let it drift downstream under the overhanging trees. We start the cast opposite ourselves or maybe slightly above and no more than 20 feet out. With a little practice, using the flip method, most fishermen can make the drift last several minutes and run out most of the fly line.

The caster has to bend down and look sideways up under the trees in order to see into the grotto. It is absolutely tantalizing to flip, flip, flip and watch the fly float back in there. Every time a fly goes back into that spot, I know it's going to get nailed. It's just a matter of time. We wait and wait and nurse the fly along, almost afraid to breathe. I love the anticipation. This is one of my favorite types of fishing.

As much fun as it is to tease trout with large salmonflies, downstream tactics are not limited to dry-fly fishing. I also use these techniques to fish nymphs.

One place where the downstream approach is especially effective is on the drop-offs. All drop-offs hold fish because the trout can rest below the lip of the drop, out of the current, and still have a steady supply of food delivered to it. Often the only approach to these holding areas, especially on larger western rivers, is from above, on the gravel bar itself. It's too deep and too dangerous to try to get out below the drop.

I have a pet spot on the Deschutes that drops off in not one but three tiers. Each of these shelves holds fish, but the third one is the best. That's where the real lunkers are, and sometimes there are steelhead, too.

To reach this spot I need a lot of line. I use the water tension method to draw off extra slack in order to get where I want to go. The water tension method creates additional slack more quickly than the flip technique and is better suited to swift-water situations.

First I cast quartering downstream using the S cast and pull back technique. Then immediately, before the slack is used up, I move the rod horizontally downstream to the side, pulling extra line out through the guides.

I always strip the extra line off the reel before I make the cast. After the cast, I swing the rod to the side downstream and the water tension pulls the line out onto the river. Once I have the line on the water, I mend it back out to the center current lanes behind the original cast.

The most common mistake when using this technique is failing to manage the slack well in order to create additional slack. You have to use a certain amount of pull to get the line out through the guides to add slack. If the line is too tight, if there isn't enough slack created in the original S cast and pull back, the horizontal movement of the rod will pull the tip of the line and the fly. But if there is a buffer of slack, the tip of the line is protected.

Many inexperienced fishermen fail to anticipate when the slack is going to run out. They wait until the last minute, when the initial slack is pretty well gone, and then try to create more

To create slack with the tension method keep a small reserve of slack at the reel after the initial cast.

Move the rod tip to the side, drawing the extra line out through the
guides.

Mend the slack this creates by moving the rod to the side, out onto the
main current behind the fly.

slack. Instead, they end up dragging the fly. I suggest you create extra slack quickly. Don't wait. In faster water, the slack is absorbed rapidly. When using the tension method you need to be decisive – don't hesitate.

After you understand how to keep a good slack buffer between you and the fly, you can repeat the tension method again and again to get extended downstream drifts. I think you'll be surprised at how far out and down you can fish with control. It's a marvelous feeling to drift a fly long distances into those hard-to-reach places.

On my pet gravel bar, there's an extremely fast current. I don't even like to wade all the way down to the first shelf. The current is just too pushy, and the gravel is constantly digging out from under me. I have to manage the line really well to get the drift where I want it to go. But when I get there, my effort is usually rewarded. I've seen more monstrous backs and fins and huge boils out on that shelf than anywhere else on the river. Unfortunately, because it's so far out and the current is so fast, I miss a lot of fish. I lose more after a short but spectacular run deep into the backing. Nevertheless, even though I don't land many fish off the gravel bar, something exciting always seems to happen. It's an explosive spot that can't be reached by any other approach but downstream.

Not all downstream fishing situations are suited to S cast tactics. An alternative to the S cast is the skitter and drop.

I first learned about the skitter and drop from an old geezer named Bill. Bill was a veteran fisherman who liked to keep his secrets to himself. When I met him on the path, he would palm his fly to hide it. If he saw me watching him fish, he would alter his tactics to try to confuse me. Bill did his best to keep other fishermen in the dark.

One day I managed to sneak up on him without getting caught. I was on a cliff above where he was fishing. I saw him before he got wind of me, so I hid in the bushes to watch.

There was a major caddis hatch on. Bill seemed at first to be fishing quite normally. He cast the fly quartering upstream and then fished it on a standard dead drift down in front of him. But at the end of the drift, he pulled back on the fly. It was like the

In the skitter and drop method of creating slack the initial cast is made quartering upstream.

As the drift proceeds a belly will form in the line downstream. The fly will soon start to drag.

As soon as drag begins, raise the rod tip, skittering the fly upstream toward yourself – but don't pull too hard or you will jerk the fly off the water.

Lower the rod tip and drop the slack that was created by skittering back onto the water. By repeating the skitter and drop a series of drifts can be created below the caster.

pull back in an S cast except that it was done a little more crisply and sharply in order to overcome surface tension on the line and fly.

The fly came skittering back upstream and in slightly toward Bill. He dropped the rod tip and fished the fly down and away. He repeated the skitter and drop three or four times before he would cast again. He was fishing in a fan pattern below him. He would repeat the skitter and drop until the fly was fishing straight downstream, then he would cast again quartering up.

It was an extremely effective technique. Bill was covering a huge amount of water, and he was being very efficient about it. The fly was on the water in a fishing zone most of the time.

To top it off, the movement of the fly was also very effective. The caddis around Bill were dipping and bouncing on the water. When he skittered the fly, it dipped and bounced, too. No wonder he was catching so many fish.

"Thanks for the lesson, Bill!" I called, not being able to resist one-upping the old man.

"You son of a bitch!" echoed from the river.

But the lesson isn't quite over. In order to do the skitter and drop, it is necessary to practice a little. You need to get a feel for how hard to pull back.

When you pull back, you do so straight toward yourself. If you overshoot it a little bit, you're going to wind up wearing the line and fly around your head. It seems to be a necessary part of the learning process. Everything has its down side, and line around the head is the down side of the skitter and drop.

Just don't practice the technique around wise-guy friends. Bring the skitter and drop out in public only after you've worked on it for a while on your own.

With practice you should be able to skitter the fly upstream to your casting position and then drop it and fish it away. You will become very efficient in your coverage of the water and especially effective when the insects are bouncing and dipping.

The skitter and drop is also a very helpful targeting technique for conventional downstream casts. The S cast and pull back approach can at times be difficult to fish to a specific target; you lose a certain amount of control during the pull back. Over the years I've worked out a couple of slight variations to the skitter and drop.

If you have a fish rising in a specific spot under the bushes below you, you may choose to cast out into the river beyond the target lane and then pull back to it. You can cause the fly to skitter across the lanes; when it gets to the right one, drop the rod suddenly and the fly will drop too.

It takes a little anticipation; the fly drops a bit behind the rod tip, but it's not at all difficult to get the timing. The fly can be lined up very accurately, then dropped drag-free and floated right into the fish's lair. I work this little tactic quite often above logjams, too.

Whenever you use skitter and drop techniques, you should use very bushy high-floating flies. The fly is not refreshed very often with false casting. When it's bouncing and skipping, it's in almost constant contact with the water. A low floater will sink almost immediately.

The caster can help the drying process by getting a good skitter with the rod tip high and then dropping suddenly. The fly will be set on top of the water rather than pulled across it to position. A fly that is set on the water floats much better than one that is pulled to a stop.

If you are using the skitter and drop in an area where there are very distinct fast and slow current lanes, you may find it useful to mend the line in such a way that it's all in a single current lane above the fly. When the line is across current lanes – especially current lanes that are varied in speed – there will be a tendency for the line to pass the fly and create drag. That's easily avoided if the line and fly are in the same lane.

The skitter and drop can also be adapted quite successfully to nymphing downstream. When fishing with a heavily weighted nymph, it's not a good idea to cast overhead. Instead, you can pull back and skitter the nymph to you, drop the rod tip, and feed slack with the tension or flip method.

On local Oregon rivers, whitefish quite often will come in below the fisherman, attracted by the debris knocked from the riverbottom. Beginner fishermen who have never had an opportunity to catch very many fish can get some practice at hooking and landing by floating a nymph downstream to the whities.

On the San Juan River in Colorado, this technique is also used somewhat unscrupulously for trout. There it's called the San Juan shuffle.

When you begin to explore downstream technique, you'll find that there are a thousand variations on the theme. It's a technique that is easily adapted to a variety of fishing conditions. As you work with downstream tactics, you'll come to find many new ways to use them.

5

Slack and
Tension Control

When I'm using slack line, sometimes there are days when the fish are there but my touch is off a bit and I just can't hook 'em. Again and again they'll bump the fly. I'll nick them but just won't get a solid connection. It's frustrating, although those days when there are no fish at all are even more frustrating.

A slack liner is always faced with the problem of how loose to fish the fly. How much slack is the right amount? If you don't use enough slack, your fly will not look good to the fish and it will be ignored. You'll make a bad presentation. On the other hand, if there is too much slack, you can end up like me on those off days: You'll attract lots of fish but won't hook any of them.

The best presentation is the one in which the line least influences the fly. Ideally, you'd simply drop a fly on the water and let it travel at the whim of the river. Then it would look as natural as an artificial insect ever will.

But fly fishing is a trap for trout; without the string to the trigger, it doesn't work. So while it is important that the fly be allowed to drift with minimum influence from the line, you still must keep control. You're still trying to catch fish.

How then do you determine how tight or loose to fish the fly? How do you judge the right amount of slack? Unfortunately there is no one right answer. Some days the fish may be easier to fool than others.

On one of my favorite rivers, there's a twilight caddis hatch that comes off right around the end of August. Just at dusk the bugs fly. A reasonable imitation is required, but you can present it almost any way you like.

It's a perfect kids' hatch. You're forgiven a multitude of sins. Just get the fly out there, and you'll have a fish on your line in seconds. Children love it. I really believe you could trip and fall face first in that river. As long as you get your fly out, you'll catch a fish.

The hatch is only a half hour long, and sometimes it gets so intense that I'll rig more than one rod with the same fly. If I break off a fly or bugger the leader, I can just put one rod down and pick up the other.

At times like this, slack line presentation is not very important. It's better to keep fairly direct contact with the fly so you're ready when the fish hits.

On the other extreme, there are days when slack and presentation mean everything. Once in a while you'll find a big old lunker way back in a logjam. No other fish are feeding, but this one has such confidence in the impenetrability of his lair that he doesn't give a darn. He's out and about.

You know up front he's the fussiest fish on earth. It's a situation in which no mistakes are allowed. You'll be forced to use every slack line trick you know to get a drift to him. The fly has to be skated and danced through the logs, and there will be slack all over the river. With any luck everything will come together at the right moment with a rise of the trout.

Between these two extremes is your average, day-to-day fishing: some slack, some tension—a balance.

The first question in achieving balance is what sort of slack pattern to create in order to get the job done. How large a coil of slack do you need? Should you use a bounce cast or an S cast? Do you need small squiggles or great big ones?

In every fishing situation, the specific conditions and the objective you wish to achieve are what dictate the size and shape of the initial slack pattern.

If you're casting downstream, the fly is traveling away from you; slack is being absorbed and you need a larger pattern to compensate. Here you should probably use a powerful S cast with a large pull back.

If you're casting upstream, the line is coming toward you; slack is being created and you need a smaller pattern of curves. Perhaps nothing more than a soft leader will do the job.

When casting across current lanes, the variation in speed between the lanes is the deciding factor. If one lane is very slow and the other is very fast, a more extreme slack pattern is needed. If the currents are similar in speed, a less severe pattern will work.

On occasion, particularly in downstream fishing, you may be in a situation in which you desire to gain control of a slack pattern at a particular point on the river. Say, for example, you're fishing to a trout off at a distance. It may be necessary to add excess slack to float the fly to the fish's position. In this case, you would sacrifice control for a portion of the drift and regain it when the fly reaches your objective. This type of fishing requires the most slack of all.

But be careful not to overdo it. Always use the least amount of slack necessary to get the job done. Don't use an S cast when a soft leader will do. Don't add a whole gob of slack using the tension method when a couple of flips will do.

Once the initial slack pattern has been created, it must be fished through. Now the focus moves from slack to control. You must find the right amount of tension to maintain slack but still be in contact with the fly.

I generally can achieve the proper tension by keeping a roughly 90-degree angle between the water and the line where it comes off the tip of the fly rod. If the angle is less than 90 degrees, I'm starting to put tension on the line. The weight of the fly line will begin to exert a subtle pull. If the angle is greater

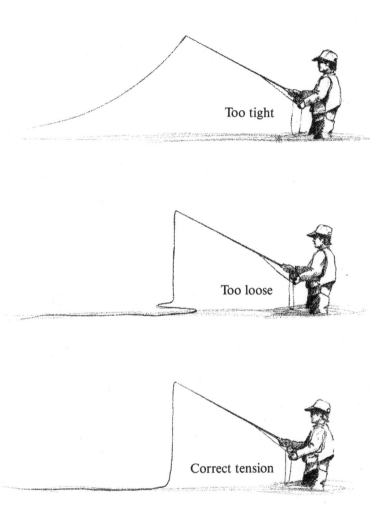

To find a good balance between slack and tension, maintain about a 90-degree angle where the line comes off the water. Less than 90 degrees will tend to pull the fly; the line will be too tight. More than 90 degrees will create unnecessary slack. It will deaden contact to the fly without improving the drift.

than 90 degrees, the line starts to puddle. There will be useless coils of slack on the water that only serve to dampen the connection between me and the fly. These coils will have to be drawn out before the hook can be sent home. The system is deadened without gain.

Please remember that the 90-degree angle is only a rule of thumb. The ability to vary and adjust is important. The right-angle rule is a stepping stone, a good place from which to begin. In the end the objective is to develop a feel for what is right – a sense of how much tension to apply.

The easiest way to maintain tension, to actually execute the control, is by putting the rod up over your head. This technique is called high sticking. High sticking is most commonly associated with nymph fishing, but it's also effective with dry flies.

When you high-stick, you cast the fly quartering upstream. As the fly comes toward you, you raise the rod, taking slack off the water. When the fly goes past, you drop the rod again, feeding the slack back in. Normally you'll raise the rod and your arms somewhat – but not all the way – to absorb slack. Most anglers like to leave a little bit of stretch in case they get a strike at the highest point of the maneuver.

With this simple technique, you don't have to strip line in and then feed it out again. It's a very efficient way to manage line on shorter casts, and the technique makes it easy to maintain a right angle.

Perhaps the only disadvantage of high sticking is that if you try to manage too much slack, you'll get caught at the top of the lift with nowhere to go. Every once in a while I get too enthusiastic about how much slack I can manage and wind up with the rod and my arms as high over my head as they'll go. This compromising position guarantees that a trout will strike. The indicator goes down, the fish is swimming around with the fly in his mouth, and I've got no way to set the hook.

My friends love it. I usually end up stumbling backward in the river trying to take up slack. The results are always the same: fish on for a moment, fish off. It gives them all a good belly laugh.

High sticking with a dry fly is usually not as extreme as high sticking with a nymph. The angle at which the leader enters the

The simplest method of controlling tension in a drift is called high sticking. The cast is made normally, quartering upstream.

The rod tip is raised to control tension as the fly comes downstream toward the caster. It is lowered again as the fly moves away.

water down to a nymph is much steeper than the angle across the water to a dry fly. If you tried to high stick a dry fly as high as a nymph, you'd quickly exceed the 90-degree angle and start pulling the fly. Nonetheless, although the amount of slack that can be controlled with a dry fly is not as great as with a nymph, it is still enough to be valuable.

A wonderful companion to high sticking is rod reach. While the angler is lifting the rod and line, he should also be following the drift of the fly down the river. As the rod goes up, it is also moving to the side.

Many fishermen are a bit lazy about stretching out and getting the most from every drift. The farther you reach, however, the more control you'll have over the slack pattern and the better the presentation.

My friend David Soares is fun to watch. He gets the absolute maximum out of every drift. Sometimes at the end of a float he looks like the Leaning Tower of Pisa. He puts his arm, his rod, and his whole body into the effort to get just a few more inches.

A drift can be extended by stretching to the side. Better fishermen put their whole body into the effort to get every inch out of a drag-free float.

He works hard to hold off drag till the last possible second. And he catches a lot of fishing doing it.

I'm convinced that longer drifts catch more fish. The farther the fly floats, the more exciting it seems to become for the fish, because the longer a fly is on the water the more helpless it looks. Therefore, the greater the distance the fly travels, the more likely the fish is to react. Stretching to the side to extend the drift will increase strikes.

Another method for extending the drift is to follow slack patterns rather than the fly.

At the end of a typical drift, a belly starts to form in the line downstream. Many anglers ignore the belly, and as they swing the rod downstream, they follow the fly. They do this with good reason. Many writers and fishing coaches have said to them over and over again, "Point your rod tip at the fly." But this admonishment is not entirely true. To get the maximum drift, you should instead follow the slack pattern. There is a subtle difference.

When you follow the fly, you are actually holding back slightly, encouraging the formation of the belly just a little sooner than need be. You hold the butt of the fly line upstream, which slightly increases curve in the line. As the belly forms, it begins to make a U shape. If you follow the slack pattern instead, you will keep your end of the U open longer. You are still moving the rod with the fly, but you're pointing slightly farther downstream, thereby floating the fly a little farther and increasing your drift by a few feet.

Saving a few seconds and a few feet of drag may not sound like much, but when all of these techniques are combined – high sticking, side reach, and following the slack pattern – they amount to a good deal. A fisherman who is conscientious can add from 3 to 6 feet to the end of every drift. Over the course of a day that's significant additional exposure – well worth the effort.

Most of the techniques discussed thus far work well with shorter casts, but the range of a cast quite often will exceed what can be controlled simply with high sticking and moving the rod to the side. In these cases, you'll have to strip line in order to control tension.

Stripping line is relatively easy as long as you have the right

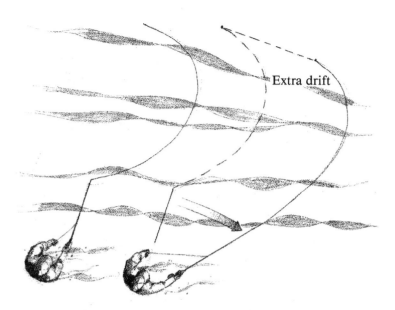

Extra drift

Many anglers follow the fly with the rod tip but the drift can be extended by following the slack pattern instead. Move the rod tip downstream slightly ahead of the fly, keeping the slack pattern open. It is slack or the lack of it that creates drag, not the fly.

hand position. If you don't use your hands correctly, it can become quite confusing. Never strip line from above your rod hand. Instead, develop coordination between the rod hand and the line hand. Hold the line over a finger on the rod hand – index or middle finger, it doesn't matter. As you draw the line in from behind the rod hand, pull it over the finger. With each strip of the line, clamp down the finger while repositioning the line hand.

By using this method, you always have a grip on the line. No matter what part of the stripping cycle you're in, if a fish takes, you still have control. Simply close your finger and strike.

This hand position is very important in fighting fish, too. I would venture to say that as high as 50 percent of the anglers I meet on my guided trips will hook a fish and immediately reach to the first guide to strip line. That's a great idea for a moment. You get a lot of line in a hurry. But when you go for the second strip, it's really a problem. If you didn't draw the line over a finger, you have no way to clamp off. Suddenly you're waving the rod around in the air trying to get hold of the line. It's awkward, and you're out of control. A lot of fish are lost this way.

After every cast, you should immediately draw the line over the rod hand finger. It should be instinctive. Always work the line from behind the hand and over the finger. When you have that drilled into your head, management of the line will become second nature.

You'll have to practice this line hand coordination and train yourself to do it. Strip, clamp; strip, clamp; strip clamp. With the right position, you can move as much line as you need and always be in control.

Often all three control techniques – stripping line, high sticking, and rod reach – can be used at the same time. Together they form a very smooth and efficient line management technique.

Even with all the tools for controlling slack, sometimes you'll still get caught with more line on the water than benefits good

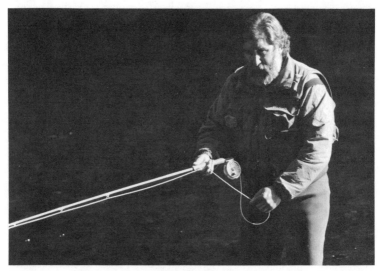

Train yourself to strip line from behind your rod hand. Draw the line over your finger to maintain control.

Drawing line straight from the first guide without drawing it over your rod hand is very ineffective . . .

. . . leading to a loss of control and a struggle to recapture the line. Many fish have been lost as a result of this simple mistake.

control. When this happens, it's important to know how to strike with slack in the line.

Almost everyone likes to go up overhead when they strike. A fish takes your fly, you're excited, your hands go up. It's a very natural reaction. Unfortunately, it's not a good reaction. It's better to use the rod horizontally over the water and strike to the side.

If you strike upward, you must lift all of the slack that's on the water in order to move the fly. Often you simply don't have enough room overhead to absorb that much line. But even worse is the time delay. It takes time to get that slack off the water. By striking upward you slow yourself down.

If you strike horizontally, there are two benefits. First, you can strike against surface tension. If the line is left on the water, a sharp crisp pull on the butt end will translate all the way to the tip end. Surface tension keeps the line from moving to the side. The hook can be sent home even when there are curves and slack in the line. Second, you can absorb more slack. You have

Striking overhead limits your range of motion. It is sometimes difficult to get all of the slack out of the line.

greater rod reach to the side. Overhead, you can raise the rod to vertical but no more. Horizontally, you can swing it all the way around behind you.

The direction of the horizontal strike should always go into the curve of the line. By striking into the curve, you're placing the most direct pressure on the line.

For some anglers it is at first confusing as to which way to go. The strike changes during the drift. If you're nymph fishing at the start of the drift, you mend up, the curve of the line is up, and the strike is up. As you approach the lift and the high stick position, the curve of the line begins to change from upstream to down. The strike moves downstream as well.

Once you've practiced a few times, the mechanics become second nature. You'll strike in the right direction without even thinking.

Sometimes striking to the side can cause you momentary panic. If there's enough slack, you may lose some control. The hook will be set, but because you had curves in the line, you

Striking to the side allows you to take up more slack. Water tension will also help you set the hook.

don't have a tight line to the fish, which is swimming around all by itself.

I don't feel this problem affects catch rate very much. I'm a firm believer in catch and release and barbless hooks – I've been using barbless flies for years. Fish *do not* simply shake off barbless hooks. If you get the hook home, the fish is not going to get rid of it.

If you have too much slack when you hook a fish, usually the fish will be very obliging and quickly take up the excess line. The minute you sting one it runs. But once in a while you get the odd guy that makes it really interesting by coming right at you. Your strike indicator is flying around the river showing where the fish has gone, and you have no control whatsoever. I once had a fish go right between my legs that way.

Even if you're out of control for a while, eventually you'll get caught up. Nine times out of ten, if the hook was set well, you'll land that fish in spite of having lost control in the middle of the process. I caught the fish that went between my legs, and I cherish the memory all the more for the high comedy.

As your skill grows with these slack and tension techniques, you'll find yourself slipping farther and farther out to the edge of control. The dream is a fly that floats the river without influence of the line or leader. That is the perfect presentation. We want to try to get closer and closer to that ideal until the line seems to be gone completely. In order to do so, we keep adding more and more slack. Some days we go over the line – we use too much slack. We hook 'em and miss 'em. We have to rein ourselves in and tighten up. But we'll keep trying.

Every time I hook a fish and don't land it because of slack line, I say to myself, "That's one I wouldn't even have *seen* without the slack."

The ones I take on the very edge of slack line control, the ones that nobody else can get to, are the ones that make me say to myself, "Yeah, I did that well." I cherish those fish the most, because they offer the greatest challenge.

6

Curve Casts

I have an odd little sidearm hitch in my casting. I used to worry about it and tried to correct it. I've since mellowed. I decided it's really not that important to keep the rod in one position; whatever is comfortable is OK as long as you're able to make adjustments when the need arises.

The sidearm crept into my casting because I try to maintain a casting stroke built around utility and not around looking good or casting mileage. For utility, I want the rod to be able to move; I don't want it locked into a single position at vertical.

For example, if I need to get a fly under an overhanging bush and I can't drift it there with a downstream presentation, I may need to lay the rod to the side almost horizontal to the water in order to fit the loop of the line into the narrow opening under the trees.

I also wouldn't want to use a vertical cast if there were an obstruction at my rod hand, say a bank of teasels. In order to keep out of trouble, I'd need to cast the rod on the wrong side, over my head, with the line working back and forth on my off shoulder.

It is flexibility of the rod position – not being locked into one pose – that allows you to advance to the next step: making curve casts. The advantages of being able to throw a curve into a fly line should be immediately obvious.

Not long ago I was fishing a stretch of river with some friends. We came to a logjam. The water off the face of the logs was fairly deep and it was very brushy up above, so I couldn't float a fly down. The only way I could fish the logs was by wading out into deep water at the lower end of the jam and casting up and around the corner to get a drift.

I used the positive curve cast. With it I was able to tuck the fly around the corner and lay it right next to the logs. It took a couple of drifts, but eventually I was able to tease out a nice 14- or 15-inch brown trout.

The positive curve is little more than a horizontal bounce

The positive curve cast is nothing more than a bounce cast thrown from a sidearm position.

cast that comes across the caster's body.

A bounce cast thrown from a vertical position has a tendency to tuck under at the end of the cast. It curls down when the bounce occurs. If you're using a weighted nymph, this tendency is even further emphasized. Sometimes a strong bounce, thrown with a weighted nymph, is called a tuck cast. The tuck is used to create slack to help sink the fly.

If the tuck or bounce cast is thrown from a sidearm position, the tuck does not go down—it goes across. That's all there is to a positive curve cast. It's an overpowered horizontal cast.

The amount of curve is controlled by the power of the cast in the same way you would control the amount of S curve in a bounce cast. The more you power the cast, the stronger the curve. A little more gentle touch, and you'll make a curve that's not quite so severe.

It's such an easy cast and so natural that it will become a well-used part of your casting arsenal. I've wondered sometimes if my sidearm casting stroke is a function of natural position or if

The extra power in the positive curve cast causes the line to snap to the side across the caster's body.

it appears because I like to use the positive curve so much. When conditions are right, I'll throw a positive curve almost every cast.

Perhaps the most obvious place to employ a curve is when casting to rising fish along a current lane in midriver. The water where the fish are feeding is faster than water closer to shore. With a positive curve, compensation for the different current speeds can be made without further adjustment. No mending is necessary.

Curves are also very useful in fishing pocket along the banks. Not far below the Pump House Hole, there's a brushy bank that's fun to fish during the summer caddis hatch. The caddis swarm around the bushes and the fish follow.

On this bank the brush is so thick it rakes the water. There are no openings to float flies under the bushes. Instead, you must pick fish out of the pockets and gaps along the edge of the brush. Here there's a premium on casting accuracy. A misplaced fly would be lost. You can't wade in to pick stuck flies out of the brush without spoiling the run, and the fish don't come out from the brush to take flies.

The positive curve cast seems made for this spot. The fly has to be curled slightly downstream when it lands, because the water right against the brush travels slower than the water in the main current 6 inches out. The pockets are small and there's no time to make mends, so the cast must penetrate the face of the brush and be set up when it touches down.

I always feel especially good when I've fished that bank well and managed to curl the fly into every nook and cranny along the shore. The fish in there aren't big, but there's a special pleasure in the way they're caught. The positive curve, even though it's easy to use, has a rewarding degree of subtlety built into it.

I could give more examples of places where a positive curve is useful, but I'm sure you'll find plenty of your own opportunities.

Once you get the hang of it, the positive curve just seems to roll off your rod tip. You'll be using it without even thinking about it. Watch out — you may start to develop a sidearm habit of your own!

The only drawback to the positive curve is that it's one-sided.

It's very easy to make curves across your body, but the opposite cast, called a negative curve, is much more difficult to do with any consistency.

In many situations where a curve would be the ideal tool, you're caught because the curve you need would be the negative one. The best compromise is an alternative way to make curves called the reach cast.

In previous discussions of the S cast and pull back technique, I emphasized that after a cast has been delivered – after the rod snap has occurred – the caster is free to manipulate the line. With the S cast, the manipulation is a steady draw back on the line. With the reach cast, you manipulate the line side to side.

The reach cast is done by aiming the rod at a target, creating rod snap, and then immediately moving the rod to the left or right in order to lay out the desired curve.

Don't hold the line tight as the rod moves to the side. Fly line should be running out through the guides. It's almost like painting with the rod tip. You send the fly to its target and then paint the curve, laying down line with a broad sweep of the rod.

The reach cast is not quite as efficient as the positive curve, but you can use it in either direction.

Because of its flexibility, casters often don't think of the reach cast as a curve cast. It actually is a curve – and more. You can make a curve, a squiggle, or a straight line; this cast will produce a variety of slack patterns. A practiced reach caster can almost lay the line 90 degrees in front of him if desired.

The key to good reach casts is to develop a freedom of movement. The rod is now allowed to move off vertical, and after the rod snap, you use it to create patterns on the water – patterns of slack that will respond to the river.

New casters first learning the reach cast typically wait too long after the rod snap to begin the reach movement. It should be done almost in one motion: The cast goes toward the target, and then immediately the reach moves to the side. Any hesitation will be translated into a straight section in the curve of the slack pattern.

Once you've mastered the skill and you have freedom of movement of the rod, you'll be able to handle a wide variety of

The reach cast is begun from a normal rod position. The cast is made straight toward the target.

fishing situations with much greater ease.

At one campground there's a spot where the water comes down a short, bouldery drop and runs into a pool. At the bottom of the drop, as it runs through the boulders, the water is split into a dozen or more current lanes, which have very different speeds. In a couple of spots there are actually suck holes or back currents that are going upriver. Any dry-fly cast across these lanes will drag instantly.

To fish this piece of water, the fly line has to be laid in a single current lane. I like to wade out one lane away from where I want to fish. I cast right up into the foam at the bottom of the drop and then, with a reach, paint the line down the current lane below where the fly has landed.

The reach allows me to fish the current lanes one at a time. I move out slowly, keeping the line and fly in a single lane, being careful not to get across the currents. I'm usually able to sneak a

As soon as rod snap has been created the rod is moved to the side, drawing a curve as the line runs out through the guides.

few fish out of an otherwise impossible situation.

Don't try to fish a long way out when using the reach or curve cast; try to stay close and get good control. Distance is not part of the game, and these techniques are not as valuable at long range. With time the little curves and reaches will become an automatic part of your casting repertoire.

The real, working reach cast is done with fairly small manipulations of the rod. It's quite subtle. You may not at first realize that a caster is using it.

My old buddy David Soares is a great reach caster. If you get lined up and watch him cast from either straight ahead or straight behind, you'll see his rod continuously playing games in the air. It doesn't go straight back and forth but tilts and flares at the end of almost every cast. It's not a powerful or overstated motion; it's just a little subtlety David has in his casting. With almost every cast he demonstrates some element of a reach, usually a subtle reach that reacts to the river currents.

If you ask David what he's doing, he'll answer, "Hell, I don't know. I'm fishing."

Watch David fish his pet runs. He moves over a little to get better position. Then he'll throw a cast with just enough reach to curl the bottom of the cast 3 feet to one side. David's little subtle curve puts the line on the opposite side of a major current lane. He gets the drift that fishermen using a straight cast do not.

When David fishes down a stretch of river, it's amazing. He hits every nook and cranny—every conceivable piece of holding water. He works the rod and line and the water continuously, getting an effective float into places that never get fished.

When David comes through a campground, he's like the Pied Piper—he picks up a gang of followers. Many of the less-experienced fishermen are not catching fish, while David is hauling them out one after another. He's always generous. He gives away flies and fixed leaders. On most days he has someone under his wing—a protégé. Even though everything David has to offer is given freely, only a handful of fishermen ever learn the most important lesson—that of reading and reacting to the water.

David's subtle addition of the reach cast—the little fine-tuning—makes a good drift excellent. It separates the mediocre fisherman from the true expert.

David is not doing anything exceptional in the way of casting. The skills are not difficult to learn. Doing reach casts is well within the ability of the average fisherman. Nonetheless, most people think that there has got to be some great secret. But the fact is, it's just good basics. Good slack line presentation. Positive curves and reaches are workhorse skills that you can use just about every time you fish.

The negative curve, in contrast, has a very limited application. You won't need this skill as often. It is perhaps more valuable as a casting exercise than as an actual fishing tool. It does have its place, however, and from time to time it may be the only way to get a fly where you need it to go.

I present it here as a more advanced technique—a test of your ability. If you're not immediately able to do the negative curve cast, don't worry; just keep practicing until you get it. Since

The negative curve cast is more difficult to throw. It is begun by casting an open loop in the sidearm position.

By dropping the rod tip suddenly, the open loop can be collapsed and placed on the water in a negative curve, away from the caster.

it's not an enormously valuable tool, you're not at a huge disadvantage if you can't do it. In my case, it was a long time from the day I first learned about the negative curve cast until I could do it with consistency.

Two things are important in order to make a negative curve: loop control and an extremely well-tuned soft leader. Unlike most of the casts discussed so far, the negative curve relies on an open loop. The negative curve is thrown from a sidearm position just like the positive curve. The idea is to create a large, open casting loop in the sidearm position, and then kill the cast before the loop unfolds, thus creating a curve.

If you lay an open casting loop on its side, the rounded candy cane shape is a curve in the negative direction. When it arrives at the appropriate position, you drop the rod tip, which suddenly takes the energy out of the cast, allowing the curve to settle on the water.

It takes a certain touch to get everything right. It's very easy to overpower a negative curve. An overpowered negative cast will convert instantly to a positive cast. The casting loop completes its travel, and the fly lands 15 feet from where you were aiming it.

To make the cast a little more manageable, I like to bring my rod from a low position and move it up. It's something of an underhand throwing motion.

A cowboy friend of mine does something he calls a rodeo cast. He strips out 20 or 30 feet of line and makes it into a lariat in the air by rotating his rod tip around in a circle.

"Yahoo! I'm going to lasso a trout," he shouts.

This whole exercise is worthless except that what my friend is creating is a great, open loop. The circular motion of the rod tip makes a huge, round circle out of the line in the air—a perfect curve.

I employ the bottom half of his rodeo cast in my negative curve; by sweeping from underneath upward, I am able to accentuate the open loop. I feel this gives me better control. I'm able to watch the curve develop, and then drop the rod when the cast is positioned properly.

The other secret to making a good negative curve is an extra-long, extra-soft leader. When I see a negative cast situation coming up, I stop and readjust the leader before I do anything else. I'll add 6 inches or more to the spaghetti leader and deliberately make it so it doesn't turn over properly. After all, in this situation I don't want the cast to turn over completely. A good, soft leader helps immensely.

Several major disadvantages of the negative curve should be fairly apparent from the onset. First, it's hard to do. A second disadvantage is lack of power. Because the cast employs an open loop and a soft leader, it has almost no power in the air. If there is any wind, you can't throw a negative curve cast; it's strictly limited to situations in which the wind is not blowing at all. A third disadvantage is that it's difficult to aim. It's hard to collapse the loop at a specific spot, and therefore it is difficult to get the fly to a target. You may find yourself casting repeatedly trying to get one drift right.

Despite these disadvantages, when you finally do get the negative curve right—and you hit the right situation—it's really fun.

Just below Beaches cabins there's a deep hole along the opposite bank. At the end of the hole there's a gradual tailout. There are almost always fish rising there. The smaller ones are straightforward, relatively easy to catch, but the larger ones play the currents, getting on the inside of a tricky little current lane.

The current sweeps along an overhanging bank for some distance; then, as the pool tails out, the river widens, leaving a seam of quiet water just inside the current lane next to the bank. The larger fish take this preferred lie, where the food is concentrated and they don't have to work as hard battling the current.

The spot is not approachable from above or below. The negative curve is the only way to get a fly inside that current with enough slack for a few seconds of drift. The fly has to be well downstream of the line.

The first time I managed to sneak a curve cast into that spot, I caught three nice fish. I was so proud, I kept fishing for almost an hour after the last fish had quit rising. It was delightful to watch that fly float so nicely in an impossible lie.

Very often when you get a negative curve cast to work, you'll be far more impressed with the cast than with the fish.

The curve cast and reach cast are very underutilized tools; there are many fishermen who do not use them at all. When you develop these tools and realize that the fly rod is not restricted to straight overhead, you'll open up miles and miles of new water that you hadn't been able to fish in the past.

7

More Complex
Slack Situations

There are almost always complex currents in the back eddies. The water twists and swirls, sometimes going one way, sometimes another. Often the current changes with the pulse of the river, shifting from one minute to the next. But the slower-moving waters and the concentrated food supply also attract trout. Eddy fishing is a special game.

To heighten the excitement, in clear water you can often spot fish. You can get above and watch them tip up, sip a fly from the surface, settle back down a foot or two, and cruise waiting for the next morsel.

Approaching fish like these can be enormously frustrating. These trout are spooky. Anytime a trout is near the surface and not covered with choppy water, it's thinking about overhead predators such as eagles and ospreys. Little things like shadows, ripples, or any unnatural movement will send the trout scurrying.

Under these conditions, any badly thrown fly – even one that's dragging only slightly – is going to put fish down. So the eddies challenge the fisherman's creativity.

Sometimes a single way of creating slack is not enough; it may take a combination of methods, and you may need to use more than one tool at a time to create your own casts in response to a particular situation. Flexibility in your casting technique allows you to take more than one approach to a problem; you can create solutions by combining tactics.

Not far below Dry Creek there's a spot where the current flows around the curve of a rocky embankment, ducks under the edge of an overhanging alder, and then sweeps toward the center of the river, leaving a large eddy swirling back.

There are fish all over, especially out along the main current line. On good days I've seen twenty or thirty trout rising. But the best fish always seem to be at the top of the eddy just under the overhanging alder.

It's quite the spot to fish – almost an eddy within an eddy. There's a fast outside current, and just inside that there is a rolling current that is the eddy line. Finally, there's another lane going upriver on the inside close to the bank and the angler. The fish like to hang out in the center of these conflicting currents.

A positive curve allows you to get the tip of the fly line to float back up under the brush. If that's all there were to it, the curve cast would be enough. But in this situation the inside sweeping current close to the angler grabs the back portion of the fly line and the fly drags instantly, spooking the trout as it goes.

A reach cast laid off to the right will handle the sweeping current. But alone it's not enough to handle the tip of the line. You get a drift, but the fly never gets back under the brush.

This situation calls for a combination of the two casts. You need to first do the curve and then the reach. These two casts can be combined because the curve cast is delivered at the moment of rod snap. It's a sidearm bounce; at the moment of delivery, the curve has been created. But at that moment the line is still in the air, which leaves the caster free to do a reach.

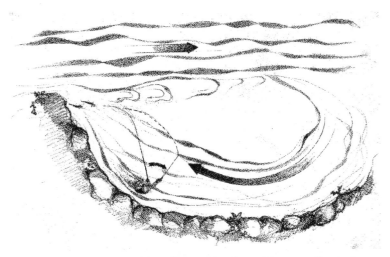

In complex situations casts can be combined to achieve specific results.
An eddy I know on the Deschutes requires a curve cast to control
the tip of the line in the outside swirling currents, combined with a
reach cast to control the body of the line in the near currents.

With the casts combined, you bounce, or curve, and tuck the
fly right up under the edge of the brush, then reach off to the side
as far as the rod tip will go.

When you've created the right slack pattern, the fly will be
suspended among all those currents drag-free for a moment.
There's not even a hint of microdrag.

When the cast is correct, the big lunker seems incredibly
foolish. He takes the fly without hesitation in a deliberate head
and tail rise. It's interesting how foolish the fish in the complicated lies actually are. It's almost as if they were daring you to get
a fly to them. They don't seem to think you can do it, and they
feed recklessly. I've always enjoyed the challenge of such trout.

I use a different combination of casts in another, much
smaller, eddy. In this spot, there's a ledge that drops off into a
deep hole. On the left bank at the top of the hole is an indentation
with the swirl in it. This little eddy is not more than 4 feet across,
but it goes around in a hurry.

During hatches there's a large trout I've nicknamed Walter

who likes to move up out of the deep water and into the back of the eddy in order to feed. From above—the only place from which I can fish to him—there are multiple layers of fast water going back and forth between me and the trout.

To get a fly to float where it needs to go, I get close to the bank and above the eddy and cast downstream with a curve that delivers the fly to the eddy's bottom. From this position, with enough slack, the fly will go around the back of the eddy and right up to the fish.

Here I combine the curve with the S cast and pull back in order to create that little extra bit of slack. With this combined cast, I am able to sneak the fly around the corner far enough to get back up to the fish's position.

A third combination of casts might be a bounce cast and then reaches both left and right, all in one cast. There's an interesting eddy near the Rock Pile where I occasionally use this combination.

In this eddy the fish are especially visible. The first look from the high bank is a heart-stopper. When the fish are in and feed-

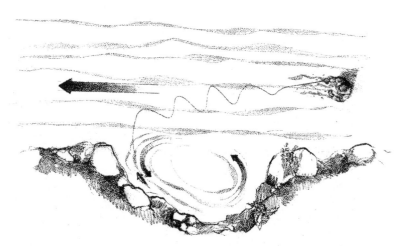

A small teapot eddy I know is fished by combining a curve cast to deliver the fly to the bottom of the eddy and an S cast to allow enough slack to drift the fly around to the fish.

ing, it's like looking into a hatchery pond, except that these are all 15- to 18-inch native rainbows.

The current patterns at the Rock Pile are quite subtle. It's not a fast-moving eddy, but the currents come and go with the pulse of the river and the swirls change constantly. They come in waves of water. The fish move about, following pockets of food on the face of these waves.

A bounce cast is necessary because the currents are somewhat unpredictable. A reserve of slack is needed to compensate for unforeseen shifts toward the center of the eddy. At the same time, the way the large flows move, there are often two or three current speeds between the caster and the trout. After I've cast across these currents with a bounce, I paint back and forth with the reach.

The idea is to counteract the currents by creating a reserve of

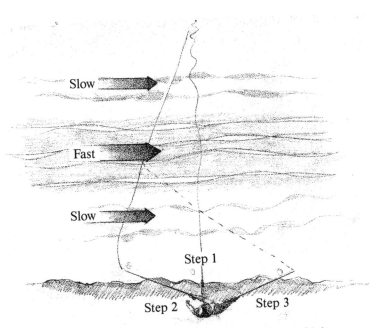

In a large eddy, fast and slow currents are overcome by combining reaches to the left and to the right. The currents are counterbalanced by painting a reversed or mirror image of the current with the line.

slack and a belly in the line that moves up the faster current lanes and down the slower ones. The uneven current speed will then bring the line back to straight while the fly is floating for a few minutes drag-free.

It's tantalizing to see the fish watch the fly while you watch the slack being absorbed.

Fish are not in a hurry here. They cruise over slowly and look at the meal closely. They know the fly is trapped and is not going anywhere. They take their time to be sure there's nothing artificial about it.

When the slack pattern is created well, the fly will remain suspended long enough to overcome the trout's caution. They tip up slowly and take the offering in a very deliberate rise. Then the biggest challenge is to keep from getting too excited. I have to contain myself so I don't rip the fly off the water before the fish actually gets his mouth around it.

On occasion, your best effort to combine casts – to beat the currents in the eddies with slack – may not be enough. If the currents are just too complex, it's sometimes better to go with the flow than to fight it and try to create an incredible slack pattern.

When I simply can't get a perfect drag-free float and I'm still suffering a tiny bit of microdrag and a lot of rejection because of it, I often go to a two-fly system. I tie on a small nymph as the point fly and a dry-fly version of the same insect on the dropper.

The dry fly acts as an indicator showing me where the nymph is. Sometimes it will attract trout, but more often, when the drift is less than perfect, the fish will reject it and pick up the nymph.

This technique works because most subaquatic forms of common insects have at least some swimming capability. Trout have far greater tolerance of movement by a nymph than by a dry fly. Offering the subsurface imitation may be enough to turn the fish on.

Combining casting techniques is often the solution to complicated currents in the eddies, but it certainly is not limited to that type of fishing. There are also many situations out in the main river that call for a multifaceted approach.

Additionally, the idea of combining techniques is not limited to casting techniques. Sometimes you need to consider other tactics, such as position, along with the right cast to get the desired result. Position is something many fishermen don't consider. Yet the spot where you stand can very dramatically affect your fishing – especially if you're a slack line fisherman.

It is well known that the first cast is the best one. A well-delivered first cast always catches more fish because it comes out of the blue – unsuspected. Each cast after the first tends to reveal the fisherman in one way or another. The fish see the leader, the drag on the fly, the spray of the cast, or the movement of the rod. Every time you present the fly you present yourself to some degree.

Position, in the simplest case, may be nothing more than moving close enough to get well within casting range so that the cast – a bounce cast, a curve cast, a reach, or whatever – is done well the first time.

This is a sharp contrast to the relatively common approach of going in guns blazing (and flies dragging), casting until you get close enough to finally present one well. In this scenario, by the time you finally present the fly well, you generally present it to empty water because the fish have already gone.

In my guide business, I've always put a great deal of effort into positioning my clients very carefully for the best results. It used to bother me when a well-positioned client would start moving around and repositioning without thinking. In the end I found this habit of shuffling so common and my frustration so regular that I decided it was time to change what I was doing. Now I position new clients several feet back from where I want them. Nine out of ten will advance 3 to 5 feet to the right spot while they're stripping line and getting ready to cast. It's kind of an involuntary reflex that most casters have.

You need to consider carefully what your position means in relation to the cast before you fish.

Say, for example, you were faced with casting across complex current lanes. If the current speeds are divergent enough, it may be very difficult if not impossible to get a drift. Here you should reposition so that you are either directly above or below the current lane, casting straight up or down it. This would simplify

Complex   Easy

Many fishermen work too hard at the game. Try to simplify at every opportunity. Don't make a complex curve cast when a few steps one way or the other can make it a far simpler direct cast.

the cast needed from a complex curve-reach combination that responds to the currents to a simple bounce or S cast that can be thrown more easily and with greater accuracy.

I believe that you should be able to make a complex cast when the situation calls for it. That is, after all, the point of this book. Yet on the other hand, you should keep things as simple as possible. Just because you can make a complex cast doesn't necessarily mean that you should. I try to uncomplicate fly fishing at every opportunity. If I can make a cast easier by taking a few steps one way or the other, I guarantee I will do it.

There is an old skiing axiom, "Never show all that you know to the mountain." Good skiers hold something in reserve so they'll have more to give when the going gets tough. The same thing is true in fly fishing. Don't try to show everything you know to the trout and the river. Use only as much of your skill as you need in order to get the job done.

The idea of threading a tiny bit of fur and feather onto the end of a gossamer string in order to attract one of the most shy and wily creatures is complex enough. There's no point in making it any more complicated.

You can also use position to control what's going on behind you. In many complex casting situations, the currents are not as big a problem as the surrounding obstructions. Trees, rocks, and high banks are the fly-fishing versions of sand traps and water hazards. They limit access and often make things substantially more difficult, if not impossible.

A mile or so above Wizard Falls, a brushy bank overhangs an underwater pile of broken rock. There's a drop-off on the outside into deeper water. It's trout heaven.

The area is concealed behind a wall of brush. I first spotted it from the other side of the river while standing on a cliff overlooking the drop-off during a green drake hatch. When I saw the fish coming up, I realized for the first time what a great run it was. I was inspired to work a little harder to find ways to fish that water.

I persisted until I found several places from which, by combining the right position with the right cast, I could get at the fish. The best spot, the one I consider the most creative, is a rock pedestal. Here you're standing on a rock 10 feet above the water, with bushes below and in front of you that you must cast over. When you hook a fish, you have to get down off the rock and crash through the bushes to the river in order to land it.

The cast is made through a natural slot in the trees and bushes. Once you get over the psychological barriers, it is relatively easy to make a short positive curve cast up around the bushes to the trout. While you're fishing, the fly is around the corner out of sight. You hear a fish take rather than see it.

I once took a very inexperienced friend to that spot. This woman had not fly-fished more than a few days in her entire life. I showed her where to stand and taught her how to make the cast, and she caught half a dozen fish without any further assistance. She was living proof that the cast was easy. It was the position that was complicated.

If you consider your position carefully, you may find ways to do things that others think are impossible. You may find places to fish that other people are not getting to. Keep adjusting until you find the right spot.

Getting the right combination of casts and techniques in super-complex situations often calls for practice. The fisherman who is familiar with a set of currents will do better than one who is attempting a cast into a new spot for the first time. There is something to be said for the home river advantage.

Each situation I have described in this chapter is one that I've fished repeatedly. The solutions to the problems were not developed in a single visit.

All guides watch one another to try to steal ideas. The better guides all have pet places—places where they've worked out a special technique.

One guide in our area, Roger Carbone, is especially good at rooting out secret spots. We watch each other quite closely. Roger has a couple of places that I can't master like he does.

One in particular comes to mind—a run along a rocky bank. It seems like every time I go by that spot, Roger's client has a fish on. But when I stop there I can't get the same results.

Roger has found something—a twist in the current or a way to make a fly get in where it's supposed to be—that I haven't been able to discover. One day I'm sure my persistence will pay off, but for now it's Roger's secret spot.

In the meantime, I've got a couple of places that Roger can't master. A few years from now, I'm quite confident we'll both have new pet places. Part of fishing – part of slack line – is the process of experimentation and learning.

This doesn't necessarily mean that you have to be on a familiar river to be successful. When I stumble onto a complex situation on a new river, I'll go ahead and fish it. Usually I end up botching the job. I make a clumsy attempt and put the fish down. But that's not the end of it.

Once the fish are down, I'll take a moment and work with the currents. I'll play with the situation until I am able to get what I think is a good presentation. Then I'll leave.

A few hours later, or perhaps the next day, I'll come back. After a practice session and a little experimentation, I usually get the result I was not able to achieve on my first pass through.

Slack line casting in complex situations is a matter of being patient, persistent, and creative.

Perhaps the best example of a complex slack cast developed over time is one that my friend Jeff Howard and I created for the slot at Canyon Creek.

The slot is a large pool perhaps 20 feet deep. It's crystal clear water, and you can see big trout at the bottom of the hole. Everybody in our area knows this place; most have been frustrated by it at one time or another.

For years Jeff and I couldn't figure it out either, but we treated the Canyon Creek slot as a learning ground. We just kept after it. Little by little we improved, although there were many frustrating days. We shot some home video one day when we were learning how to get a fly into this place. The tape definitely should be censored for language. Shot after shot showed one or the other of us climbing a tree to get a fly back down. But at the end of the video there is a fish – a very nice one.

To do the cast Jeff and I finally figured out, you must skirt a tree on the backcast and then lay the line right up alongside a bush with a reach cast to the left. If the cast was aimed well, with any luck it will land in one particular lane of current – the sweet spot. If it does, you must immediately follow with a series of mends to give the fly enough slack to sink all the way to the bottom. Once down, you keep feeding line with the flip method.

At this point, the fly goes out of your sight and your partner must serve as a spotter. Now it is getting hot. Sometimes the spotter will be able to see the fish moving over, getting lined up on the streamer as it drifts. Other times the trout at first ignore it and then run it down from behind. Still other times they just ignore it altogether. We keep on casting.

Over time Jeff and I, taking turns at this odd fly-fishing game, have caught a fair number of large fish. And we have certainly provided ourselves with hours of entertainment.

This particular situation is a classic example of creative slack line fishing. We combined a number of slack line skills—position, backcast, reach, mend, flip, and tension control, along with practice and repetition—to get a good presentation to a single fish. When we hook it you know we are proud.

Thus in slack line fishing, persistence and creativity pay off. We used a broad variety of skills and creative energy to accomplish what other fishermen could not. We broke with tradition in order to accomplish the task at hand. We refused to give up until we found a way to accomplish our goal.

8

Matching the Hatch versus Slack Line Control

Here's a conversation I'll bet you've been in before.

Your friend Bill, who just got back from a fishing trip, announces, "We had a great time over on the Swamp Water River last weekend. We must have caught fifty fish a day."

"Oh yeah?" you reply. "What did you use?"

It's the classic fisherman's question: What's the hatch? What are they biting? What fly should I use?

It takes only the briefest acquaintance with fly fishing to recognize that trout are selective. They eat only very specific foods. Although the choice of patterns is enormous, the number of flies that will work on a given day is quite small.

With so many options and a choice that is so critical, naturally the question of which fly to use becomes uppermost in everyone's mind.

This has led to the growing trend of hatch matching. It has resulted in some really fine books about the various aquatic insects, their identification, and fly patterns that match them. Becoming something of an armchair entomologist has become part of the fly-fishing game today.

But often, having the right fly is not all there is to catching trout. I have a couple of cagey fly-fishing friends who are masters of the half answer. They are quick to tell you the hatch. Maybe they will even give you one of their special flies. But in the best tradition of fly fishing, they do not tell all they know about how to catch the fish.

The part about how and where to present the fly is deliberately left out. They know that in more complex situations, the less astute fisherman can take the right fly to the river, cast it around all day, and probably not disturb the fish very much.

A classic example of this is salmonfly fishing in Oregon. The salmonfly is perhaps the most famous western hatch of them all. But just because salmonflies are on the water does not mean that everybody is knocking 'em dead. In fact, some anglers get quite frustrated.

They do not realize that it's not good enough just to have the right fly on the water. It has to be the right fly on the right water and in the right way. The angler has to use his slack line skill to get to where the fish live.

Increasingly in the world of catch and release, where fish have been caught and educated several times over, the game is becoming more sophisticated. The fish demand not only the right fly but also that it is presented well.

All too many fishermen are unwilling to face this fact of fly fishing. It is human nature to want easy solutions. If someone will tell us what fly we should use, many of us are only too willing to stop there—tie that fly on; it should work. No further thought is given to presentation and the self-discipline it takes to become a better caster.

For the serious angler, choosing the right fly and presenting it well are two equally important aspects of a total approach. The right fly presented poorly will catch some trout, but it's far from being really effective. By the same token, almost any fly presented well will manage to fool the odd fish, but this is not an effective approach either.

Both elements must be present for a fly fisherman to be at the top of his game. When somebody tells me, "We had a great weekend on the Swamp Water River," I want to know not only "What fly did you use?" but also "Where did you fish it? What time of day? How did you present the fly? Was it swinging or dead drift? Was it on the bottom or over the weed beds? How did you fish it?" I know that in order to duplicate success I must have the right presentation in addition to the right fly.

Quite often fishermen will have some success with one of these two aspects of fly fishing, and their initial success leads them to become one-sided. Some insist that presentation alone is the way to get the job done, while just as many others believe that matching the hatch is the only answer to fishing success.

The "one fly only" fisherman believes that presentation is everything. This person will tell you, "I fish a number #14 Adams. That's all I ever use, and I always catch fish." I don't doubt that these single-minded people are effective after a fashion. I know they catch fish.

I have a friend whose pet pattern is a tan #16 Lafontaine Sparkle Pupa nymph. This gentleman is a very good fisherman. He casts beautifully and has a delicate touch with a nymph. He's constantly playing with weight and leader. He gets the nymph to the fish as well as anyone. On more than one occasion he has put me to shame with his little Sparkle Pupa. I cannot question his effectiveness.

Unfortunately, however, this man has tunnel vision. He works on every aspect of the fishing game except how to pick the right fly. He absolutely refuses to get involved in the match-the-hatch game.

Somewhere along the line he was introduced to the tan Sparkle Pupa. He used it successfully during a hatch period, and now it's become a cure-all. He puts on a Sparkle Pupa both when it's appropriate and when it's not. The light brown color enables the nymph to catch some fish all the time—much like a Hare's Ear.

This partial success only takes him farther down the lopsided road he's on. But in the long run, my friend has severely limited his ability to catch fish. He has his moments, no doubt of that, but he also has a lot of down time; he'll be on fire one day and cold as stone the next.

In the end, a fisherman who is paying attention to both sides of the game—to matching the hatch *and* to presenting the fly well—will have greater success. Over the course of a week, through changing hatches and changing conditions, a lack of flexibility will invariably make itself known.

On the other hand, I deplore the growing trend in fly fishing of entomological snobbery. You don't have to know Latin names to be a good fisherman. The Adams and the Hare's Ear are classic examples. These two perennially popular flies probably catch more fish in a year than all the other patterns combined, and neither is a direct imitation of anything in nature. Knowing an insect's Latin name has never helped my fishing.

The general size, shape, and color of the fly are the valuable information gained from taking the time to study aquatic insects and match the hatches. In order to obtain this information, there is no substitute for having a bug in your hand. You cannot look at insects in the air or on the water from a distance and get a decent match. You've got to take your hat and catch a bug out of the air or dig one off the bottom of the stream and look at it closely in order to know what fly you should use.

For some this may be as far into entomology as you need to go. If you catch the bugs and look at them closely, and then rummage through your boxes until you find one roughly the same size, shape, and color, you've taken a giant step toward fishing success.

Others may choose to go a little farther, however. I find the study of entomology quite interesting. Aside from fishing, the bugs in and of themselves—their habits and behavior—are fascinating. I find it amazing that there is such a detailed and diverse microuniverse beneath the surface of the streams I fish and know so well. A little further study reveals which insects crawl, which ones swim, which ones live in the riffles, and which ones live in the pools. This information can often be used for more effective fishing.

Insect knowledge can suggest motion, ways I should fish flies, and where I should fish them. It helps me understand the fish better, too. It has been demonstrated again and again that the behavior of the fish is tied to the behavior of the food.

Knowing insects is also a very useful predictive tool. I have chased down many worthwhile hatches through the back door. I discover a certain type of caddis sealed in its shell, and I know it has to come out fairly soon. By tearing the case open, I can get the pupa out and match it by simply tying up a fly. All that remains is waiting to find out when those caddis will come out of their cases.

I've had some fabulous days when I was lying in wait like that. I was prepared, with the right fly in my pocket. The instant I saw the activity I was anticipating, I knew what to do. It's a good feeling to be on top of your game that way.

The primary value of entomology is gaining broad knowledge of groups of insects that have related behavior. For example, it is useful to know that the family of clinging mayflies lives in swift riffle water and emerges from the nymphal shuck at the bottom of the stream, not on the surface. That suggests a particular fly pattern and way to fish.

On my home river, the Metolius, the clinging mayflies emerge at the same time as the green drakes, and sometimes they dominate. Only an astute fisherman who catches bugs and looks at them will discover the difference. It very definitely makes a difference to the fish. There's a period during each season when green drake fishermen get really frustrated by a lack of results.

To this day I don't know what species those clinging mayflies are. And I don't really give a hoot. All the clinging mayflies fish the same. I'm catching trout – that's all I need to know.

Another extreme in entomology is the voodoo of exotic tying materials and very precise patterns to imitate specific insects. I've found that if the flies are presented well, fish usually will accept a wide variety of imitations for the same hatch.

I recall one day on the North Platt River with Danny Byford

and one other friend. We split up and went our own way. There was a small, light-colored mayfly coming off. I tied on a light tan fly and went at it. I was having a very successful day.

A couple of hours later we all got back together for lunch. In unison we said, "Have I got the fly for you!" Each of us independently had found the key to success. But when we brought the flies out to compare them, they all were slightly different.

Each of us were using a #16 dry fly with an upright wing to imitate the mayfly, but mine was light tan, Dan's was light green, and the third guy had on a light gray one. The fish wanted #16 light-colored mayflies. That's all there was to it.

That's why the Adams and Hare's Ear work so well—they don't imitate anything specific, but they imitate a lot of things in general. General imitation is all that is necessary. That's as far as entomology needs to go.

The guy who tells me that the only fly that works is one with a pink foobober feather from an extinct pterodactyl usually has a product to sell.

Several fly shops in my local area are caught up in this kind of thing. They insist that the only stonefly nymph imitation to use on the Deschutes is a Girdle Bug. But a Girdle Bug alone is not enough. You have to have the special one that they tie in the shop. It has to be a Girdle Bug with black legs, a red head, and body of black chenille with a silver fleck. "That's the only one that works," they say.

I don't believe it. Any big, black, ugly fly will work. The Girdle Bug itself should be proof enough of that. A Girdle Bug certainly doesn't look like a stonefly. It is the roughest of imitations. It's black and it has wiggly legs—that's as close as it comes.

Exact imitation is not necessary. In any given situation, a wide variety of flies will work. Hatch matching is useful only to get in the ballpark. Almost anything roughly like the living insect will get the job done.

I have a very simple formula that I use to determine how much time and energy to spend on hatch matching and how much to spend on other aspects of the fishing game: a reasonable fly + good presentation = trout.

I believe strongly that, yes, you should be a hatch matcher.

Yes, you should take the time to do your entomology homework. But once it's done, forget about the fly and get on with the game of presentation.

The best fishermen I know don't change flies all the time. They find a fly in which they have reasonable confidence, and then they stick with that fly until they can make it do what they know it should.

Don't waste your time searching and searching and rummaging through your whole box for that right magic fly. You're better off getting a good fly and then working relentlessly on slack line presentation until you're absolutely convinced you have shown that fly to the very best of your ability.

I write a little column in our local weekly newspaper, the *Nugget*. I once wrote about the golden stonefly hatch. I said that based on my own experience, matching the hatch was good when it first came on but was pretty worthless thereafter. Any number of readers were very quick to point out the error of my thinking. It was repeatedly demonstrated to me that you certainly *could* catch fish with that fly.

It was clearly a case in which I knew the insect, I knew the fly that imitated it, but I just hadn't spent enough time on presentation to make the combination work. The solution to the puzzle was obvious; I just hadn't taken the time to fit the pieces together right.

That humbling experience has made me far more reluctant to say that a fly doesn't work. I now am considerably more careful how I fish a fly before I abandon it and move on to the next imitation.

In most onstream situations, the fish are not going absolutely crazy over a single insect. Blizzard hatches, though we all dream of them, are actually quite rare. More often you will fish a sporadic hatch, with some fish working and others more reluctant. There are fish feeding, but it's not a feeding frenzy. Under these conditions, trout just aren't quite so dumb and you have to work a little harder. There will be times when, even though you have the right fly, you don't get all the response you desire.

This is not necessarily a reason to change flies, however. Nine times out of ten, changing flies won't get you anything either. Be persistent, work on the presentation, and soon enough the cycle will change in your favor again.

Often my clients on guide trips want to move on and try something different. "Don't you think we ought to change flies?" they ask when it gets a little slow.

"No," I tell them, "not until I have a reason." I have to see a hatch change, I have to see something that makes me think my original research – the fly I chose in the beginning – is wrong. I watch the bug cycles closely; I watch for changes in the hatch; I watch for new insects to appear. But I won't change the fly until I see a change in the cycle.

In the long run, by being persistent and by working on presentation as much as I work on choosing the right fly, I seem to catch more fish. Granted, the amount I catch goes up and down during the day. There are times when I am not as effective and it's very tempting to change flies and try something new. But when I resist the temptation and focus on my presentation and on getting the right fly to the right place in the right way, if I stick with the fly long enough, I start catching trout again.

Fly fishing is a very inexact science. There are many variables: the fly, the presentation, and the trout themselves – maybe they're just not hungry right now. You can't expect optimum results all the time.

I believe the best approach is to cut down the odds in your favor. That's what matching the hatch is all about. It's a way to eliminate the randomness of choosing the fly. Then, once you've made your choice, be confident and seek other options as the variable to change.

In an inexact world, the two-sided approach – match the hatch and then present the fly well – is the best way to find that magic ticket that will make the trout respond.

9

The Hinged Nymphing System

"What's so special about your leader?" I asked. I was honestly curious, but I must have used the wrong tone. Apparently there was too much doubt in my voice.

"Nothing, nothing at all," David snapped back.

So began a summer's worth of games to find out what this new mystery nymphing leader was all about.

My friend David Renton had shown it to me briefly, and he would let me look at it from a distance while he was fishing. But about any further detail his lips were sealed.

Even from a distance I could answer my own question. The leader was special because it gave David a kind of control I had never seen before. I could read his indicator from 25 yards. I could watch it probe the bottom. I could tell the instant his nymph touched down. I knew exactly how it was behaving. The indicator was so sensitive it was like eyes on the bottom of the river. It made nymph fishing seem almost like dry-fly fishing.

Over the course of the summer, I wheedled, cajoled, flattered, and bribed. Slowly, bit by bit, I extracted the secret of the indicator.

It was a system developed by two guides out of Oakland, California, named Dean Hickson and David Schubert. Their leader and indicator method was developed in the Pit River country on Hat Creek and the Fall River.

The hinged indicator system is built from scratch. It starts with a short, stout butt section, about 4 feet long, tapered down to approximately 2X, 8 or 10 pounds. Exact dimensions are not important. Flexibility is one of the keys to this system.

Typically I use the butt section of an old dry-fly leader to make the tapered section of my nymphing leader. After a dry leader has been rebuilt into a spaghetti leader enough times, it starts to lose its taper; it becomes too thick for new tippet, but it's just right to be trimmed up as the base of a nymphing leader.

I shorten these leaders on both ends until they're down to about 4 feet. I can trim the heavy end of the leader without affecting turnover, because this is not a dry-fly leader. The butt section of a hinged leader is so short and stout that the connection is very direct.

I tie a yarn indicator directly onto the end of the 4-foot leader butt, using an improved clench knot. The type of yarn is very important; I'll discuss that in more detail in just a moment.

The indicator can be trimmed with a pair of scissors. I like to get mine down to a little ball to improve wind resistance.

The tippet material, one long piece of a single-diameter leader, is then tied on directly behind the indicator. I tie an improved clench knot right around the heavier butt section. The tippet slides back and forth, while the indicator keeps it on the line.

The length and diameter of the tippet can be varied according to conditions. I fish everything from 2X to 7X tippet–for steelhead or ultraselective trout.

The 90-degree angle created between the tippet and the butt section gives the leader system its name. It allows the nymph to

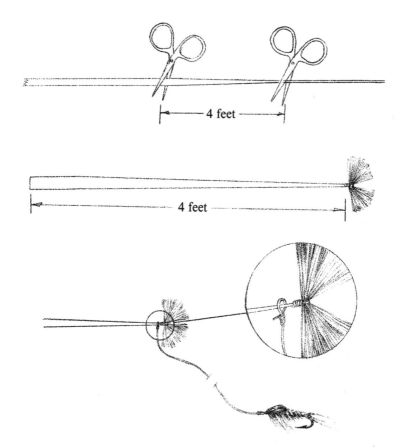

To create a hinge indicator system start with the worn-out butt section of an old dry-fly leader. Trim the leader at both ends until it's about 4 feet long. Try to get just the tapered section of the old leader. Clinch knot a yarn indicator directly into the end of this short, stout butt leader. Trim the indicator to size and shape. Create the hinge by clinch knotting the tippet around the butt section behind the indicator. The indicator will keep the tippet on the line. Length of the tippet should be a foot or so more than the depth of the water.

be fished directly below the indicator and greatly enhances the sensitivity of the entire system.

The weight used to sink the fly is also varied according to conditions. Split shot of various sizes can be applied to the leader, or the system can be fished with weighted nymphs that have lead tied into the fly body.

There are several distinct advantages to this unusual leader configuration. First and foremost is sensitivity. No other system comes close.

I first learned my nymphing back in the good, old days when men were men and we tried to frustrate each other by fishing blindly along the bottom of the river without any indicators.

I hated nymphing because I never knew where my fly was or how it was behaving unless it was hung up. To make matters worse, I read repeated accounts by various authors who had stood on a high bank and watched as trout picked up the fly of some poor ignorant slob below. The fish could pick up the fly and spit it out without giving the man any indication that they had come or gone.

What a glorious catch-22. The articles said you had to have a sixth sense as to when the fish were taking your fly. But how do you become sensitive to fish that you can't even feel? How do you develop a sixth sense for something you don't even know is happening? Yanking back on the line when the urge struck just wasn't cutting it for me. I guess I'm just not quite that far into the Zen of fly fishing.

But eventually, out of necessity, I got fairly good at probing the bottom. When conditions called for it, I could make a fair accounting of myself with a nymph. But the honest truth is that I never enjoyed it very much. Because nymphing was blind, it was a second-rate substitute – I was a dry-fly man through and through.

Over the course of the years that followed, in an effort to get more comfortable with nymphing, I experimented with just about every indicator system that came along. I started with the early handmade cork indicators, moved to the plastic ones you slide on the line with a toothpick, and then tried the rubber pinch-on ones that fall off and litter the riverbanks. I even tried various types of yarn indicators. Despite all these teaching aids, becoming a good nymph fisherman was a painful process.

Today, things have improved enormously. We have better understanding of nymph fishing and a greater refinement. Basic nymphing can be learned fairly easily using large indicators and heavy flies.

But refined nymphing – learning to fish the nooks and crannies, to probe the drop-offs, to handle a nymph with the skill of a dry-fly angler – has remained as difficult to learn as ever. Today, nymphing is at once the easiest and the most challenging of fly-fishing methods. Newcomers get started quickly, but they soon discover that they are going to spend a long, long time getting really good.

The primary reason refined nymphing is so difficult to learn is that even with a traditional indicator, you're still blind as to how the nymph is behaving. You know little more than whether you're on the bottom. It's difficult to have a clear vision of exactly where your fly is and how it looks to the fish.

But the hinged indicator system brings a new refinement to all this. When I finally pried the information out of David Renton, I felt for the first time that I was able to fish the bottom with the same kind of confidence I have with a dry fly. The indicator allowed my mind's eye to actually see the fly probing among the rocks.

For example, if I'm fishing a run with a hidden rock in it, the hinged system will allow me to draw a road map. By watching the indicator and its response to the hesitation of the nymph, I can map out the sides of the rock, the front, the back – I can fish around it with total control. When I am done, I know with confidence that I have fished that rock to the best of my ability.

No other system has allowed me the same confidence. With other indicators I can probe the area and make enough presentations to feel I've really covered the water well. But that's not the same as knowing which side of the rock I'm fishing and knowing exactly when that trout should be looking at the fly.

There are many reasons for the hinged system's sensitivity. It starts with the yarn itself. The material used in the indicator is a special kind of polypropylene yarn. Be warned: There is no substitute for this material. If you don't have the right yarn, the system will not work.

Most of the products currently on the market as indicator yarn are not acceptable for this system. The typical Glo Bug yarn used as an indicator today has very fine, straight fibers. In the hinged indicator system, this yarn will soon become water-logged. You will find yourself engaged in an ongoing struggle to keep the indicator afloat.

The fibers of the correct polypropylene are kinky, not straight. If you examine a single fiber of the good indicator mate-rial, you'll see that it is quite coarse, twisted, and curly. The kinkiness of the fiber causes it to have greater surface area and to trap air, allowing it to stay afloat better than other materials.

I get my indicator material in the craft store. I buy Maxi-Cord brand polypropylene macramé yarn. Other products may be equivalent, but you would have to do additional research to be sure. This yarn comes in large skeins, one of which is a lifetime supply for the average angler. There is three-strand and five-strand yarn; it doesn't matter which you use, because the indica-tor is going to be fluffed out anyway. The yarn costs five or six dollars per skein.

At the time of this writing there is only one product on the fly-fishing market that comes close to being correct. This is a premade indicator used in a modified version of the hinged sys-tem and marketed through Umpqua Feather Merchants. No one puts the product out in bulk so that you can make your own indicators. With the rapidly growing popularity of this new fishing method, I have no doubt this situation will change very soon; in the meantime, the angler is on his own to find sources for the right material.

I have experimented with a variety of colors. My favorites are bright yellow and pink. The bright yellow is excellent dur-ing almost any daylight conditions, and the pink works well toward twilight. Frequently I will combine the pink and yellow. These two-tone indicators cover an even wider range of light conditions.

I've also experimented with orange and white but haven't had as good results with them. White is highly visible in most light but can become confused with foam on the water. Orange shows up fairly well but simply isn't as effective as bright yellow.

Once you have the right indicator yarn, you'll be amazed at how high it sits on the water. It is virtually unsinkable unless you have the leader system rigged wrong. The yarn has so much flotation it actually is able to suspend a weighted nymph somewhat.

The hinge also plays an important role in the sensitivity of the system. Because the fly is rigged at a 90-degree angle to the line, it allows the fly to be in much closer contact with the indicator. It's a vertical fishing system. Both the indicator and the fly are in the same current lane.

The distance between the indicator and the weight should be about 6 to 12 inches greater than the depth of the water. The nymph should be able to just touch bottom. For the waters I fish, I typically have about 3 feet between my indicator and fly. In the same water, more traditional systems are rigged at 7, 8, or even 9 feet.

In chapter 2 I discussed the effects of casting across current lanes – the push-pull that currents can set up on a line and leader. When the traditional nymph rigging is cast up and across, the indicator is fished off to one side. Even with a tuck or bounce cast to add slack, you still have a leader across the currents. The fly is being pulled no matter what you do. Even though that pull is not great, it has an enormous impact. It's the nymphing version of microdrag.

Microdrag on a nymph is different from microdrag on a dry fly. It doesn't put fish off, as most nymphs are capable of some swimming action, but it does tend to slow sink rate.

To understand better what is happening, it might help to back up and think about basic physics. In Galileo's experiments dropping various weights off a tower, he found that objects of different mass dropped at the same rate of speed.

There is no reason that these experiments shouldn't also work in water. But that suggests that a heavy split shot and a light one should sink at the same rate. That's counter to fisher-

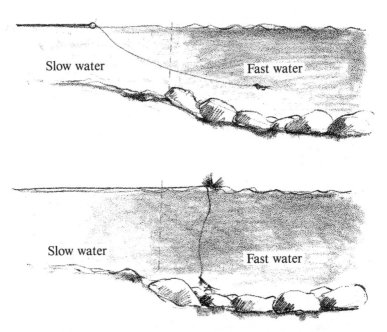

The hinged system allows much closer contact between the fly and the indicator. The traditional system fishes across current lanes, so extra tippet and weight must be added to overcome pull on the line. The hinge system fishes on the same current lane; lighter flies and shorter tippets can be used to make the system more sensitive.

men's logic, even though it is true. If you drop a large and a small split shot at your feet in the water, they will both sink at the same rate of speed.

Why then don't they sink at the same rate when they're out on the end of a fly line? The answer is nymphing microdrag. The sink rate of a split shot or weighted fly is reduced by pull on the line and leader.

To compensate, to overcome microdrag and get the fly to the bottom in a reasonable amount of time, the traditional system uses a longer leader and heavier flies. The longer leader cuts through the water better than a fly line. Because of its smaller diameter, the leader is less affected by the currents. It has less resistance. Extra weight outpowers the minute pull that remains.

If the fly is heavy enough, it will counterbalance microdrag.

The net effect of minor tension on the line and leader is to make the entire system less sensitive. You must have greater distance between indicator and fly and you must have heavier flies to drag the system down to reach the bottom.

On the other hand, the hinged system uses slack more efficiently. The indicator is not fished off to the side; it's on the same lane as the fly. The leader and fly cut through the vagaries of the river better.

Of course, this doesn't happen automatically. You, the caster, have to make the system work properly to get the desired result.

When cast, the hinged leader system turns over effectively down to the indicator. At that point there is a large step down in tippet size from 2X (approximately) in the heavy butt section to 4X, 5X, or even lighter in the tippet section. This large step down causes the leader to collapse at the indicator. From that point down it piles on the water.

This excess slack in the leader allows the fisherman to mend the indicator directly above the fly. This mend of the indicator is critical to fishing the hinged system. I'll talk more about the techniques for making this mend in chapter 10; for now let's look at how it affects the presentation of the fly.

The mend places the indicator above the fly but on the same current lane. At this point the fly or split shot has no pull whatsoever on it. It drops like a rock, sinking immediately to the bottom.

If you fail to make the mend and leave the indicator below the fly, the system will fish more like a traditional leader. Sink rate will be slower.

The reason for this phenomenon is that upper surface layers of a river always move faster than those near the bottom. Friction of water on the rocks creates an effect known as the boundary layer, which means there is slower-moving water close to the bottom and faster water at the top.

Therefore, an indicator on the surface will always move downstream faster than the fly, which is in the slower-moving deeper layers. If the indicator is downstream of the fly, it will start pulling. But when the proper mend is made and the indica-

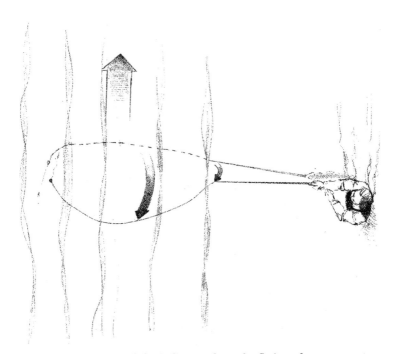

It is important to mend the indicator above the fly in order to promote
rapid sink rate. The indicator on the surface travels faster than the fly on
the bottom. Therefore, an indicator left below the fly will pull slightly,
greatly reducing sink rate. An indicator mended above the fly will not
pull; the fly drops immediately to the bottom.

tor is positioned above the fly, it will overtake the fly, creating
slack as it comes. This is a perfect situation, and the fly will go to
the bottom without a hitch.

I often demonstrate this effect to clients by taking the leader
in my hand and dropping it on the river at our feet. First I'll set it
up with the indicator below the fly. As the system floats past, we
can watch the fly settle slowly to the bottom.

Then I reverse the indicator and put it above the fly. The
effect is dramatic—the fly is on the bottom almost instantane-

ously. The minor pull of the leader, which seems like nothing at all, is enough that it takes 6 feet for a fly to settle to the bottom with the indicator below but only 6 inches with it above.

Over the last several years I've introduced the hinged system to many people. Some like it and some don't. Almost without exception, those who don't like it don't mend. They don't understand the importance of the indicator's position. Without the early mend, the hinged leader system is not much different from any other fishing system. It's probably not worth the bother. An early mend made immediately after the cast is absolutely crucial to fishing the hinged system effectively. It sets up what is to follow.

Once the fly is down, the situation changes. Drag starts to play a different role. The indicator begins to guide the fly down the river. Microdrag turns from an enemy into a friend.

A weighted nymph or split shot, if it were left alone, would just sink to the bottom and stop. It would quickly wedge in the rocks. Something is needed to help move it along. Microdrag takes over this role.

We often talk about dead-drifted nymphs, but what we commonly call a dead-drift presentation in nymphing is actually a stop-and-go action. The nymph grabs the bottom for a moment, starts to hang up, and then is moved forward by a gentle nudge from the line and leader. The nymph is traveling slower than the current speed, but it is being edged on down the river by a pull from the leader.

This is an extremely realistic presentation, because naturals that have been swept off the bottom are struggling to regain a hold. They grab at the rocks, often failing to get a grip and drifting on. It's a hesitating, stop-and-go movement just like the one we're producing with the artificial nymph. Fish are so accustomed to this stop-and-go action that their behavior is almost like a reflex response. They go right to the nymph. An insect that has moved but is not yet hidden is extremely vulnerable.

With the hinged system, we make this stop-and-go presentation with far greater sensitivity. The leader is pulling the fly from above, it's in close contact, but the indicator doesn't have enough pull to draw the fly away from the bottom. The pull doesn't lift the fly back up into the water column; it's just enough to nudge it along.

The fly bumps along the gravel, stopping and then being pulled by the indicator. It's as if your fly is rolling along the bottom with a little balloon on a string trailing to the surface showing its every motion in detail.

With practice, from the surface you'll be able to tell the instant your fly touches the bottom; you will see the indicator stall out and slow down. It will have a telltale flicker action every time the nymph bumps the bottom. The tip of your fly line will slowly drift past the indicator, which is being held back slightly by the fly on the riverbottom.

The entire leader is almost like an automated fishing system. This is why it lends itself so well to slack line fishing. The fly bumps along the bottom, reflecting its travels to the indicator. The fisherman just keeps a little bit of slack between the line and the indicator to allow the system to drift down the river undisturbed. It isn't until the slack runs out between the line and indicator that the fly lifts and swings away from the bottom.

Sensitivity is not the only advantage of the system; the hinged leader is also extremely flexible. When the sensitivity is coupled with flexibility, the system can be fine-tuned to make presentations that simply are not possible with other systems.

There are three primary variables that can be adjusted easily: indicator size, tippet length, and fly or split shot weight. All three are interrelated and must be balanced.

I adjust the indicator size based largely on the water type and fly weight. In slower, more delicate situations I'll use a very small indicator; in rougher water with larger flies I'll use a larger one.

Near my home there's a pleasant little fishery called the Crooked River. At certain times of the year it gets quite low, below 100 cubic feet per second. The fish congregate in weedy channels between the boulders and feed on little, green scuds. The flow is slow enough and the channels shallow enough that it only takes one or two turns of very fine lead to weight the fly properly. I make an indicator ball about the size of a pea, using a single strand of three-strand macramé yarn.

At other times, in the early spring, when the stonefly nymphs are migrating in the heavy waters of the Deschutes, I will double up the material and use two full pieces of yarn, six strands, to make an indicator ball the size of a quarter.

Once the indicator size is set for the overall conditions, I generally don't fool with that adjustment very much. An established system is pretty well fixed from the fly line to the tip of the leader butt and the indicator. In fact, it's so permanent that if I'm not moving from one body of water to the next, my nymphing rods often stay rigged with a single indicator for weeks at a time. I use rod cases that hold both rod and reel. I cut the tippet off, reel the indicator to the tip-top, fold the rod, and stick it in the case ready to go for next time.

Tippet length is much more variable. It is the most important of the three adjustments and needs to be worked constantly as you move from shallow to deep water and back again.

My rule of thumb is that a tippet should be 6 to 12 inches deeper than the water being fished. Tippet that is too short won't allow the fly to sink to the bottom; it won't get to the fish zone. Tippet that is too long deadens the whole system and allows the fly to stop too long on the bottom.

The indicator can let you know what needs to be done. If the tippet is too short, there will be no flickering motion of the indicator caused by the nymph bumping the bottom. The tip of the fly line and the indicator will travel down the river at approximately the same speed, because the riverbottom is not holding the nymph back.

If the tippet is too long, the system will have a dead feel. The nymph starts to grab the riverbottom too strongly. There will be hang ups and the indicator may stop flickering and takes on a steady drag; it may even begin to sink and act waterlogged. But with the right material, the indicator will not become waterlogged, and as soon as you shorten the tippet, the indicator will become responsive again.

It is often convenient to make tippet adjustments by breaking into the system at the indicator rather than at the tip. By cutting the tippet where it is tied into the main leader, behind the indicator, I can either take out a little bit of tippet material or splice in a short piece in order to adjust the system without the hassle of retying flies and crimping on new split shot.

The last of the three adjustments, fly weight, frequently needs to be worked in conjunction with tippet length. When the early mend is made properly, fly weight doesn't have very much to do with getting to the bottom, but once the system is being fished, it has a lot to do with keeping the fly down.

Pull from the indicator on a sunken fly will be greater in faster water than in slower water. Then, a slightly heavier fly or split shot and longer leader may be needed to keep the fly solidly on the bottom. It does not need to be as heavy as the fly used to sink a conventional leader, but it needs to have a little more weight than a fly used in slower water.

Take care not to use flies that are too heavy for the system, however. A fly that is overweighted will slow down too much and can cause the system to act very much like it was being fished with too long a tippet. Everything becomes sluggish. You'll sink the indicator or make it unresponsive, and the fly will be stuck on the bottom and not bump along.

The most interesting part of weight adjustment is how this variable can be used to create specific effects with a nymph—effects too delicate to be performed with other systems.

There are some circumstances in which you might like to fish the fly a little way off the bottom. Some rivers may have nymph species that drift for long periods of time suspended above the riverbottom. Or there may be cases when you would like to drift a nymph just over the top of a weed bed. To do so, you can shorten the tippet and achieve a balance between indicator size and nymph weight that will allow the fly to hang vertically below the indicator, suspended in the water column.

To fish this way, you must learn to look for rollover of the indicator. When the fly is suspended straight down below the indicator, at the moment the weight comes onto the leader it causes the indicator to roll over on the surface of the river.

When cast, the indicator lands randomly on the water. It doesn't matter which side is up. It will float that way until the weight of the nymph pulls on the knot. At that point it rolls over until the knot is down. With a little bit of practice, you'll quickly learn to identify the rollover and understand that it means the nymph is in the vertical position fishing.

When fishing suspended like this, you need to experiment to find the right depth. Lengthen the tippet until you find the bottom (or the top of the weeds), and then shorten back 1 or 2 inches.

Another effect I've found useful is one I call the moon walk. By adjusting indicator, tippet, and fly, I can cause the nymph to lift slightly and then fall back instead of drifting stop-and-go in constant contact with the bottom. It will tap the bottom, float for a distance, and then tap again.

This tactic has been especially effective for me when I fish various types of emergers. During major hatches, fish see the bugs escaping the bottom and heading toward the surface rather than being in the natural drift trying to regain the bottom. The moon walk, which is not quite so tight to the bottom, is a better presentation in these cases.

Finally, sometimes you may wish to really drag the bottom, creating more of a crawling effect than the usual stop-and-go. For example, if you locate a stonefly migration route during the salmonfly prehatch, a nymph that is really gripping the bottom, appearing to crawl, is a better imitation than one that tends to drift.

These effects, all of which are very useful at one time or another, cannot be duplicated with other, less-responsive systems.

The hinged system also lends itself to fishing two flies. A high percentage of the time, I'll use a large, weighted dropper fly, such as a stonefly or crawdad imitation, to add weight to the system. Then I'll add a smaller point fly that is generally representative of the hatch at the time: mayfly, caddis, or possibly a midge. This system is much more productive than fishing dead weight on the line, such as a split shot, which has no possibility of hooking a fish whatsoever.

I tie a dropper on by cutting the tippet at the point where I wish to add the second fly. Then I splice the tippet back together with a blood knot. I leave one of the tag ends on the knot a little longer than usual, tie the second fly onto that tag, and cut the

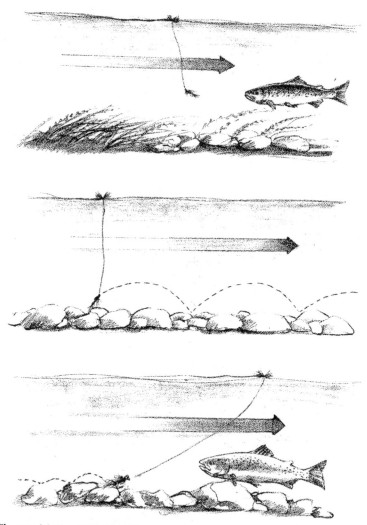

The sensitivity of the hinged system allows for fine adjustments. By lengthening the leader and changing the weight of the fly, a nymph can be suspended above the weed beds and the bottom; "moon walked" along the bottom, creating an emerger look; or crawled along the bottom to look like insects trying to regain a foothold in the natural drift.

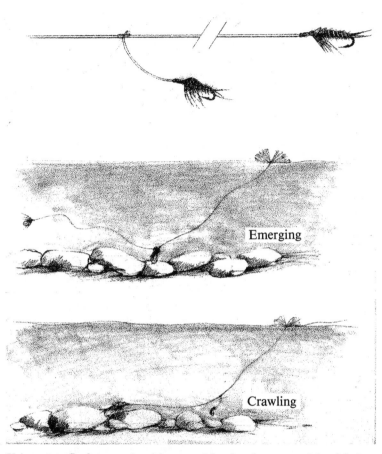

Using a two-fly dropper rig with one weighted and one unweighted fly is often better than fishing with added weight such as split shot on the line. 1. The dropper is created by tying a second nymph on the tag end of a blood knot 18 inches or so up the line. 2. By putting the weighted fly on the dropper you can create an emerger look with the lighter unweighted fly. 3. By placing the weighted fly on the point you can make the smaller fly crawl the bottom.

other tag away. The finished dropper should be no longer than 2 or 3 inches. (Longer drop leaders tend to tangle.)

Sometimes the two flies in the system will fish equally well – I'll catch as many fish on one as on the other. At other times, when fish are more selective, I'll get most of them on one fly. But every time I pick up a stray on the odd fly, I know that's one fish I would not have caught without the dropper.

Most of the time when I'm fishing a dropper I put the heavy fly up the leader as if it were a split shot. In this way the heavy fly does a stop-and-go imitation, but the smaller, lighter fly, which is more likely to be swept off the bottom, has the freedom to drift up into the water column and back. It looks more like an emerger.

On some days when nothing else is working, I'll reverse the flies, put the weight on the point, and lengthen the tippet slightly. Then both the large and the small flies grip the bottom more firmly. I'll achieve a stop-and-go look with a little, tiny fly. This unusual look cannot be duplicated with split shot alone.

There seems to be no end to the variations that can be achieved with the hinged system. I've been fishing it a number of years, and I'm still discovering what it can do and exploring its potential. It works for trout, for steelhead, and I've even modified it for warm-water fish. It has been adaptable to every type of stream condition I've encountered to date. As use of the system spreads to more and more diverse waters, I'm confident that other creative anglers will find many more new, interesting ways to use the system's sensitivity and flexibility to solve a variety of angling problems.

I urge you to give the system a good, thorough testing. I'm sure you'll enjoy it. After some experimentation, you'll be impressed by what the hinged leader system can do.

10

Water Casting and the High Art of Mending

The humble mend is such a simple technique that some might think it's hardly worth mentioning. Most fishermen do it almost without thinking. It's a very simple and direct slack technique – just lift the line and reposition it on the current where you want it. Just a little up and over motion. Once you understand how to do it, it's second nature.

Yet mending does have an artful side to it. How much lift and roll does it take? Can you be quite precise with the placement of slack created by the mend? Can you mend the line all the way to the leader without moving the fly? That's an interesting challenge – not so easy to do.

Mending is a touch cast. You need the ability to apply a very precise amount of lift and roll to the line in order to achieve specific goals.

A soft leader is a valuable aid. The S shape of a good leader

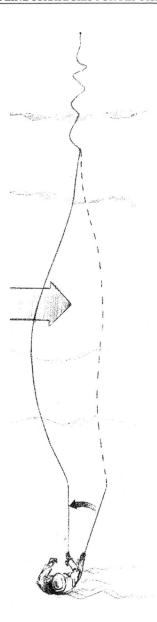

The traditional mend coupled
with a good soft leader is the
ideal way to control the rear
portion of the line. The soft
leader prevents movement of
the fly during the mend. A
simple up-and-over motion
places the body of the line on
the current where desired.

creates a buffer between line and fly. It will help accommodate less-than-perfect mends by absorbing excess energy. It's very helpful if you're trying to mend all the way to the tip of the line.

But in truth, attempts to mend the line all the way to the leader by conventional means are a bit like parlor games; they're not really practical fishing tools. The touch has to be too precise, and you miss too many casts.

Traditional mending is best suited as a technique for managing the back two-thirds of the fly line—the portion closest to the angler. You can make quick, easy adjustments to that part of the line on the current even while the fly is drifting. But there is a second kind of mending, the roll cast mend, which is a better tool for managing the forward portion of the line.

The distinction between these two techniques is that conventional mending is done from a horizontal position and doesn't load the rod. When you lift up and over, you physically pick the line up off the water. There's a little bit of flip that runs down the line, but there is no rod loading in the sense of bending the rod and taking it in and out of flex as in a casting motion. A conventional mend could be thrown with a broom handle. The length of the rod is more important than its flex or ability to create rod snap.

The roll cast mend, on the other hand, is a true casting stroke. It is done from a vertical position and has a very distinct forward motion and rod snap. The rod snap sends a loop down the line. By learning to control the amount of snap and its direction, you can make very precise adjustments of the line—clear down to the leader.

To make a roll cast mend, I first deliver a conventional cast to place the line on the water. The rod at this point is horizontal. Then I release some slack and bring the rod tip up to vertical.

This movement to vertical is very important. If you fail to get the rod tip up, or at least to a sidearm position, the cast cannot be aimed. You will flip line uselessly into the air.

There needs to be some slack in your non-rod hand in order to raise the rod without pulling line off the water. When I cast the first time, I keep a small reserve of slack in my hand, which I

The roll cast mend is an excellent tool for controlling the forward portion
of the line. A true casting stroke rolls slack down the line where it
can be positioned at the tip of the line. The roll cast mend is ideal for
managing the hinged indicator system.

release when I raise the rod to vertical. Then I clamp the line again with my finger and cast a second time.

There are two distinct casting motions. The first delivers the fly to the target, and the second creates the mend. The mend is not as strong as the original cast, but it still needs to be a good stroke with a definite rod snap in order to be effective. It's very much like a traditional roll cast motion, hence the name roll cast mend.

The size of the mend is controlled by the amount of force put into the cast. You'll very quickly develop a touch. You can make large loops or small, whatever the situation calls for. Most casters don't seem to think about it much; the right touch comes quite naturally with a minimal amount of practice.

The shape of the loop is controlled by how you aim the rod tip. The rule of casting states that where you point the tip at the moment of rod snap is where the line will go.

When you already have line on the water, however, the movement of the rod does not dictate where the tip of the line

The roll cast mend is a true casting stroke. The first step is to release slack and bring the rod to a vertical casting position.

The roll cast mend is made with a controlled power application. The amount of power controls the size and shape of the mend.

goes but where the top of the loop goes. The roll cast motion is therefore generally aimed to one side or the other, either left or right of the fly or indicator, in order to put a curve into the mend.

The roll cast mend is an extremely versatile tool. It seems to have been made for working with the hinged indicator system. In chapter 9 I emphasized repeatedly that the indicator must be placed above the fly in order to accelerate the sink rate and get the fly to the bottom quickly. The roll cast mend is how I do this.

In a typical nymph drift, I will make the initial cast to place the fly in the current lane where I want it. The hinged leader piles the cast so that the fly and indicator land together in a heap. I hesitate just a second in order to allow the fly to sink an inch or so, then follow with a roll cast mend.

With the tip of the line held by the water, I am able to throw a mend that places the indicator very precisely above the fly. With one flip of the line, the entire drift is set up.

Additional roll cast mends can be thrown at any time during

The slack created by the roll cast mend rolls down the line. This mend is a valuable tool for controlling the tip portion of the line.

the drift for greater control if the need arises. It all depends on the indicator, the fly, the currents, and the way they behave together.

The roll cast mend is also an extremely useful tool for positioning small amounts of slack quite precisely. It tends to be more specific than a traditional mend. I can put a little *pop* on the line—a very small, quick casting motion—and place precise little bits of slack in the line.

In the late fall, when the tiny mayflies hatch, there's a place I like to fish called the "idiot hole." No one knows why it's the idiot hole, but I like to say it's because the fish there make you an idiot.

There's a rock ledge down the length of the hole. The water goes from 2 feet to 20. Some really nice fish come up out of the deep water and hug the edge of the ledge to feed during good hatches.

The ledge creates a swirling current. It's like a series of minor eddies rolling along in a line. Dead drift without microdrag is very, very difficult to achieve here, hence all the idiots who go wandering away babbling about throwing fly rods into the river and taking up golf.

To get fish out of this spot, I have to use all the tactics I know, and even then there is some luck. First I tie on a good, soft leader, then I use the technique of roll cast mending. By holding the rod tip vertical and flipping tiny bits of slack at the right moment, in anticipation of the pull, I am sometimes able to thread the line and leader through the currents without microdrag getting hold of the line.

A third variation on the roll cast mend is called stack mending. By stripping line and repeating roll cast mends, you can place line on a specific current lane in midriver.

My friend Paul Petersen was the first one to demonstrate this technique for me. Paul's a great outdoorsman. He loves to catch big fish, so naturally he loves to fish streamers.

Everything about Paul's technique is big—big flies, big casts, big fish. Paul would throw his streamer as far out into the river as he could, right out in the center current lanes. He would then follow with a set of enormous roll cast mends.

With each casting motion, the rod would whistle in the stillness of the early morning air. It was very distinctive. There was a *whoosh, whoosh, whoosh* of the rod mending with every ounce of Paul's strength behind it.

With each roll cast mend, Paul would release a little more slack. He used the tension technique to add line to his cast. He would swing his rod well off to the side to draw line out through the guides, then he would mend that line with a roll cast motion out to the center of the river.

Using this technique, he was able to pile a substantial amount of line in very specific current lanes. He could create a hinged effect—a 90-degree angle in the line. With it he could hold flies out in midriver much longer than the rest of us, who were using more conventional techniques.

Paul's style of midstream presentation to the current lanes is not limited to streamers. A little more subtle version of the same technique is a very useful dry-fly tactic.

Quite often during the green drake hatch there are large

surface-feeding fish out in the center of the river in fairly swift water. These fish can't be approached with a traditional drift. But by stack mending—placing first the fly and then the line in a single current lane—I am often able to float a fly into these areas.

The initial cast is made to the target current lane and is followed by a stack mend. This sets up a downstream angle in the tip of the line and a reserve of slack in midriver. As the midriver slack is absorbed, a belly begins to form in the line. I draw out more slack by the tension method, then roll cast mend it to the original position, thus removing the belly that was starting to form.

The cast is repeated as often as necessary. With each casting stroke, the distance between the 90-degree angle and the fly is made larger. By fishing this way, I'm not dealing with the typical cross-current problems. The fly is in effect being fished as if it were straight downstream.

Stack mending is also an effective technique in nymphing. Sometimes a single roll cast mend to place the line above the fly is not enough. If I want to extend a drift to get the fly to go a little farther, I can repeat the casting motion and stack line.

The hinged indicator coupled with a stack mend is an excellent addition to the arsenal of downstream tactics. I use this combination to drift nymphs well downstream of my position. No other nymphing method will enable me to make that same presentation as well.

Because of the extra distance between the indicator and fly in a traditionally rigged system, a large downstream U forms very rapidly when the fly is fished below the angler. The line and leader must go downstream from the fly to the indicator and then back upstream to the caster. Control is lost almost immediately.

With the hinged system and more direct contact between the indicator and fly, this strongly exaggerated U shape does not form. The hinge allows you to retain control.

When that improved control is coupled with the stack mend, a whole new area of fishing is open to the angler. You can fish downstream with a nymph farther and more effectively than ever before.

On the Deschutes there are many old salmon spawning areas

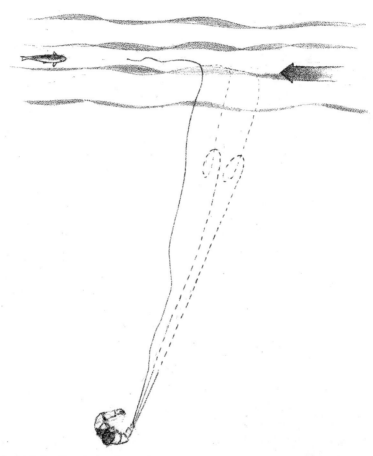

Repeated roll cast mends can be used to stack line on a distant center current lane. This technique can be used to drift a fly to fish that might otherwise be impossible to reach.

that create a washboard effect on the gravel bars. Each shelf is usually deeper and more fishy. A traditional nymphing method is limited as to how far out into these areas it can reach. But with the hinged indicator and stack mend, the deeper, farther reaches of these bars begin to open up to the angler.

Another, similar technique used to fish a bit more directly downstream is to place the roll cast mend in conjunction with a bounce or S cast. Very often you cannot create quite enough slack with the initial bounce and will find yourself running out of slack halfway through the drift. A roll cast mend targeted right at the fly can create enough slack to complete that drift.

The roll cast mend is a wonderful little utility. I now use the little quick flicks of the roll cast far more than the traditional mend.

But perhaps its most shining moment is with the hinged indicator system. It's as if these two techniques were built for each other. The roll cast mend becomes an art form when you

The slack patterns created with the roll cast mend are ideal for fishing the hinged indicator system.

see it worked to maximum advantage with the hinged indicator
system.

The little flick, flick, flick of the roll cast mend allows you to
work the fly in new and creative ways. The indicator can be
drifted and the slack controlled in ways you might not have
considered before. It's a technique that has allowed me to walk
nymphs into all sorts of new and interesting locations.

The roll cast mend is only part of a larger series of casts
known as water casts. A water cast is any cast that uses surface
tension rather than the weight of the fly line in the air to load the
rod for the casting stroke.

As I explained earlier, each casting stroke has a phase that
loads the rod. The rod has to be bent in order to store the energy
that will throw the line as the rod comes out of flex.

Traditionally, the angler puts the line up in the air on a backcast, then changes the direction of the rod and starts moving
forward again; the weight of the line, which is still going to the
rear, starts pulling on the rod. The rod bends or loads, thereby
storing energy for the cast.

An alternative way to load energy in the rod is by using
surface tension of the water on the line. This is water casting.
The roll cast, the roll cast mend, and the pickup to an overhead
position are all examples of water casts.

The roll cast, probably the best known of the water casts, is
so dependent on the pull of water on the line that it can't even be
practiced without water. You simply can't perform a roll cast off
the grass – the rod never loads.

I really enjoy using the water casts, especially when I am
nymph fishing. They're a very practical way to fish. Odd as it
may sound, I probably roll cast almost as much as I overhead
cast.

Twenty years ago, when I moved from the Rocky Mountains
to the Northwest, I had to get my roll casting down in a hurry.
The new rivers dictated it. There simply wasn't enough room
among all that beautiful Oregon greenery on the banks for a
backcast.

Since that early initiation, my water casting has grown to
more than a high-background cast – more than a way to keep out

of trouble behind. It is in and of itself a very efficient way to handle a line and fly.

There's an old axiom, "You can't catch fish with your fly in the air." I don't know what it is about conventional casting that makes us feel we've got to have the rod waving around, but most of us are guilty of overcasting. We get that old fly in the air and false cast it back and forth trying to wear out the wind.

False casting is inefficient. Huge amounts of time are wasted. Every movement of the rod is an exposure to the fish. And it always risks tangling the line or getting the cast screwed up somehow. So better fishermen always try to minimize casting; they usually make no more than two or three casting strokes per presentation. Each movement of the rod has a purpose: raising it up, changing direction, extending line, or whatever. Then, *bang*, the fly is back to the target.

The water cast is the most efficient cast of all: One stroke and the fly is where it belongs.

The tension cast is a good example of this efficiency. While fly fishing on a river, it is common to start a cast upstream and finish the drift with the fly below you. The tension cast is a very simple and direct way of getting the fly from downstream up.

To make a tension cast, I let the fly complete its swing until it is directly below me. Then I start the casting stroke by slowly moving the rod forward and lifting the tip slightly. The lifting motion does two things. It reduces the surface tension somewhat, and if I am fishing with a weighted fly, it will bring the fly closer to the surface.

If I don't start the cast with this lifting motion to loosen the line from the grip of surface tension, the loading on the rod is generally too great. I'll have a tendency to overpower the rod and not be able to make a cast strong enough to get the line free of the water.

The casting stroke follows the lift, and there should be no hesitation between the two. As soon as the line is drawn approximately shoulder-high, I turn my upper body to face slightly upriver, then I deliver the cast. The fly comes from downstream behind me to a position in front and above.

I aim the cast by pointing the rod tip at the moment of

delivery. The tension cast is very good as a change-of-direction cast. It is quite easy to make a relatively severe change in the angle of the line. A cast that starts straight below me can be delivered at an angle almost 45 degrees above.

Its ability to change direction makes the tension cast a great way to fish a traditional drift with less casting effort. I have the fly back on the water fishing very quickly. It's an extremely direct way to get from downstream to upstream, fishing again.

I have timed the efficiency of this one-cast system to compare conventional nymphing with a water-casting approach. It takes about five seconds from the time a fly has finished its swing at the end of a drift to place it upstream with a tension cast, follow with a roll cast mend to position the indicator, and sink the fly back to the bottom and have it fishing again. There is very little lost time; 90 percent of the fishing time is spent with the fly in the fish's zone.

The traditional nymphing system, casting overhead, takes considerably more time. The casting alone takes more than five

The tension cast begins with the line on the water directly downstream from the caster's position.

Bring your hand slowly to shoulder height in order to lift weighted flies off the bottom. Cast without hesitation.

The cast is delivered upstream. The rod will be loaded and the cast created by the tension of water on the line.

seconds. Then you have to add sink time on top of that. Only about 50 percent of the total fishing time is spent with the fly in the actual fish zone where a trout is likely to eat it.

There are often times when fishing is nothing more than this – efficiency. The more you show a fly along the bottom in the fish's feeding zone, the more fish you're going to catch.

Water casting is also extremely important in fishing weighted flies and indicators with split shot and droppers on the line. These systems are not the easiest things in the world to cast overhead. The risk of entanglement is far greater than with a standard dry fly.

It is therefore important to minimize the casting strokes and the amount of time that these rigs are up in the air. The nymph fisherman needs to adapt his casting technique. You should not try to cast and fish nymphs the same way you fish a dry fly.

In some circles in the fishing community, there are strong prejudices against things like weighted flies, split shot, and indicators, perhaps in part because these fishermen have not been adapting their casting to accommodate the weight and wind resistance of both flies and indicators.

Water casting is a tool to control more-awkward systems. Basic nymphing, the approach I outlined for beginners in chapter 1, is a water-casting method. It keeps beginners out of trouble, and with it the equipment is managed better than with overhead casting.

But this approach goes well beyond what beginners can do. By using a tension cast, a roll cast mend, and basic nymphing technique, I can fish with enormous efficiency. My line is not in the air getting tangled, and my fly spends more time where a fish can grab it.

I also feel that there's no loss of pleasure whatsoever in fishing with water casts. I can have as much fun with water casts and nymphs as I do stalking rising trout with a dry fly.

I like variety in my fishing. I wouldn't want to fish dries all the time, and I wouldn't want to be limited to nymphs either. I find nymphing with the fine control and efficiency produced by the hinged indicator and water casts to be very enjoyable. I can get out on good gravel bars where there are a lot of dips and drop-offs to hold fish and spend a whole afternoon playing with a nymph. It is every bit as challenging as stalking rising fish with a dry fly. Often I see the fish I'm after; I'll watch them take the nymph like it was a dry fly.

It is a very interesting experience to have a long day of fishing – one that has been both productive and fun, filled with challenges and fish – and suddenly realize I haven't put the line overhead more than a handful of times all day. I used water casting, with the roll cast, roll cast mend, and tension cast, almost exclusively. It is a unique approach but very effective.

Do not get the idea, however, that all nymphing is restricted to water casting without ever going overhead. There are times in all fishing when a little more distance is required – when roll casting runs out of range. Roll casting and tension casting are restricted to 30 or 35 feet and are not good ways to fish distance.

There is a water-casting technique called water hauling that will allow you to gain a little more range and still maintain better control over a heavy or awkward rig.

Water hauling is a way to extend line quickly without the difficulty of repeated false casting. The fly and line are brought up into the air on a backcast and then delivered with a single casting stroke forward.

You'll quite often find that this forward stroke is not very powerful, because it's hard to get a weighted rig off the water and into the air with a tightly looped backcast.

I let this weaker cast touch the water in front, but I don't let it settle. As soon as it touches the water, I use a tension cast to put it back in the air a second time. This time, because I already have the rig partially in the air and have only minor tension from the water, I can get a much better backcast. I then deliver another, stronger forward cast with a double haul that shoots line and takes the fly farther out to the target. In four casting strokes – back, forward, back, forward – I have extended line from 20 to 50 feet. Best of all, I was not required to keep that awkward weighted rig in the air for all four casts.

Often the trouble with weighted rigs comes when you try to false cast them. They will go in the air once and deliver forward fairly easily. But then when you try to go back and forth for that second false cast, the weight makes its presence known.

The only real drawback to water hauling is the disturbance it creates on the water. If there is no choppiness or broken surface to mask the haul, it will put trout down. You need to be careful where you aim the haul. But in riffle water, where there is plenty of masking, the technique is a great way to cast nymphs, weighted steelhead flies, or streamers.

All the water casts are, for the most part, quite simple to perform and very much underutilized. They are very efficient and useful in handling awkward rigs and are a quick, easy way to get the fly where you want it to go. Water casting should become another valuable tool in the slack liner's growing arsenal.

11

Slack to Set Up and Control Swing

The old fishing books, the classics like Ray Bergman's *Trout*, were filled with color drawings of wet flies. These wet flies, which have all but disappeared from the market today, usually had counterparts in the dry-fly world. There was a wet Royal Coachman and a dry. A Cahill wet or dry. The wet-fly version was tied with a softer-beard hackle and a duck quill wing down over the back tent-style.

The wet flies were not fished dead-drift like today's nymphs. Instead, they were presented on the swing, fished on a tight line with a slow movement across the currents.

Today this style of fishing is all but lost. Seldom do you see anyone on the stream using traditional swing tactics for trout. Only a few writers still talk about it. Sylvester Nemes in his excellent little *Soft-Hackled Fly* book details how to fish flies on the swing, and occasionally David Hughes will bring it up in some of his writing. Otherwise it's quite obscure.

It's a shame that the modern fly fisherman, in the rush to embrace the newer dead-drift style of nymph fishing, has all but lost sight of the value of the older tactics. Swing techniques, especially during hatches of swimming insects such as the caddis and clinging mayflies, can be incredibly productive.

On the Deschutes there is a little island, near White Horse, that I like to fish. During the summer caddis hatches, it's a hot spot, perfect for swing tactics.

The caddis hatches put a lot of activity on the water. Often, all at the same time, pupae are emerging from the bottom, adults are swimming back to lay eggs, and still other insects are fluttering on the surface.

When I fish the island, I like to try to cover all the bases. First I'll pass through the water with a dry fly. That usually brings several fish. Then I turn around and make a second pass with swing tactics. I vary the flies on the swing pass quite a bit, sometimes using a Sparkle Pupa for the wet fly and sometimes a soft hackle. The soft hackles are good because their appearance is general enough to imitate both pupa and adult. A third pattern I like is a down-wing fly much like the old-style wet fly.

To fish the wet fly or nymph in the old style, I cast either across or across and down. I usually try to give the fly a little bit of slack with a bounce or S cast. The slack allows the fly to sink an inch or two. These flies are unweighted, so they don't penetrate very far or very fast.

The second step is to set up the swing. The idea here is to bring the fly across the current slowly to make it look like an insect that is coming both across and down the current.

The fly is under tension during the entire presentation. The speed of the swing is controlled by the amount of belly you allow to develop in the line. A large belly pulls harder, a small one less. Slack mended into the line will control the amount of tension.

Too much pull and the fly rips across the currents, making an unnatural presentation. Too little pull and the fly wavers in the current in one place and doesn't look like it's swimming.

At the start of the drift, to slow the swing, I mend line up-

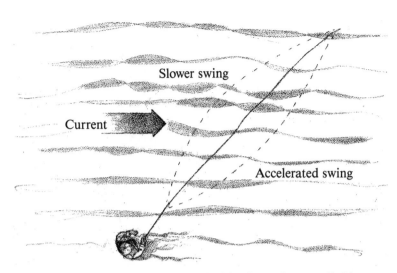

In a traditional wet fly swing the speed of the fly can be controlled by mending upstream to increase slack and slow the fly down, or by mending downstream to remove slack and accelerate the fly.

stream with a conventional mend to put slack into the belly of the line. As the line begins to swing across, I continue to mend upstream in order to maintain a nice, constant swing speed. The number of times I mend and the size of the mends will control the speed of the swing.

On occasion, if a swing is too slow, I may need to change the direction of the mend. A downstream mend will add belly to the line, increasing tension and causing the fly to move a little faster.

Judging the right speed is a matter of practice. I generally like to swing the fly as slowly as I can without stalling. I want it to swing across the currents, but I don't want it to stop. The movement should be slow but steady.

This style of fishing is exciting, because the strikes on a swinging fly are hard and fast. The fly is under tension, so there is very direct contact between the angler and the fish. There is not the customary slack buffer as in dry-fly or nymph fishing.

It's important that you don't react too hard. The fish will generally hook themselves or they won't get hooked at all. Setting the hook only serves to increase the pressure on the leader, resulting in break-offs and lost fish.

In order to buffer the strikes from large fish, I often keep a drop loop. I pull a small amount of line off the reel and hold it with my finger. When I get a hit, rather than striking, I drop the slack, thus buffering the impact of the fish on the line. It takes some self-discipline to learn not to strike and to let line go. It's a very unnatural reaction. When a fish comes unexpectedly, it's startling; it jolts you into striking. But keeping a soft touch and resisting the urge to strike back will result in more fish on the line.

On my little island, the second pass – the wet-fly pass – is easily as productive as the first run through with a dry and often is even more fruitful. Many times I come away with double the number of fish hooked and landed, and usually the biggest fish is on the wet fly.

There are some variations on the wet-fly theme that can be very productive, too. Sometimes I like to fish wet and dry in a single pass. I may decide to do this with two flies or with one.

If I choose to use the two-fly system, I will set up a dropper rig. The wet fly, usually a Sparkle Pupa or other swimming nymph, is tied on the point. A dry fly is tied on the drop.

This system is cast quartering upstream exactly like a standard dry-fly presentation. The drift is made in the usual way, except that the dry fly now acts as both a fish attractor and a strike indicator. Fish may be inclined to take either fly during this dead-drift phase.

As the dry-fly portion of the drift comes to an end and the fly is ready to start dragging, I make an exaggerated upstream mend, pulling the flies toward me. This sets up a wet-fly swing. With any luck, I have pulled hard enough to drag the dry fly under. In the second phase of the drift, it will be fished as a wet fly.

The mend also serves to reposition the belly in the line. The fly moves directly into a swing. I continue to mend as necessary to control the swing through the rest of the drift.

This technique is limited to riffle waters that will mask the repositioning of the fly. That, however, is not a problem, since swing tactics themselves generally are most effective in shallow

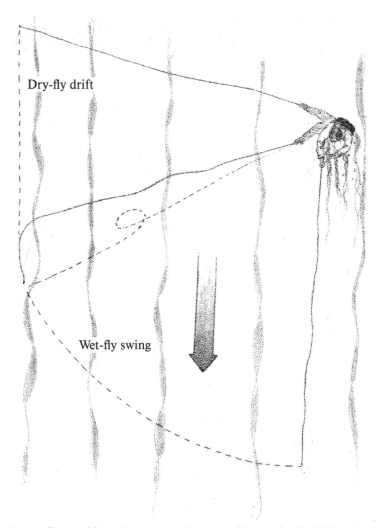

Dry-fly drift

Wet-fly swing

An excellent caddis technique combines a traditional dry-fly drift with a
controlled wet-fly swing. The fly is cast upstream and fished down
dead drift as a dry fly. As it starts to swing the caster applies a roll cast
mend. The mend is slightly overpowered in order to draw the fly under.
The drift is continued as a wet-fly swing.

riffle waters during hatch times, when fish are already inclined to be more aggressive and less easily disturbed in their feeding patterns.

The primary advantage of this system is that you can see and feel what you're doing. I use a good floating fly that will be a highly visible marker in the dry-fly phase of the drift.

An alternative, more subtle, variation on this system is what I call damp-fly fishing. I deliberately choose a fly that is not a high floater. The Cul du Canard (CDC) caddis, or duck butt fly, as it is sometimes called, works especially well in this application. This fly is tied with a feather from around the duck's preening gland. This feather is coated with the duck's natural oil. There are several styles of CDC caddis. The ones I like are very simple, just a dubbed body and a CDC wing.

The CDC has several advantages. The natural oils tend to trap air, and the fly becomes surrounded in a sheath of bubbles. Also, the fly is easily restored to floating or semifloating condition with a single backcast. Finally, the CDC wing, once it is wet, flows back over the fly. It becomes nothing more than a slightly modernized version of a very old-fashioned wet fly.

Despite the oils (and things some writers have said about CDCs), these caddis are not high floaters. The fly will start the drift dry or slightly damp, in the film, but by the end of the drift they are usually under.

Because they are half sunk in the first phase of the drift, the flies are often hard to see. The angler must be very attentive and must be prepared to strike if there are any unusual movements in the riffly water. The fish do, however, usually show themselves with a boil.

The second phase of the drift walks the CDC caddis into a swing. Much as in the two-fly technique, I mend up to reposition the line above the fly, then swing it through the drift exactly like a traditional wet fly.

The distinction of this technique is that with a damp fly I don't need to pull the fly under, so I try to be a little more subtle in the transition from dead drift to swing. I use more mends and try to make the transition without a pull.

By fishing the fly in transition, from dry to damp to wet-fly swing, I am able to show the fish a variety of looks during a single presentation.

The advantage of the damp-fly strategy is that the transition from drift to swing is a particularly attractive movement for fish. A high percentage of takes occur as the fly moves from one phase to the other.

This change of movement – the transition from dead drift to swing – is also very important in nymph fishing. As a nymph moves along the bottom dead-drift, it often will attract attention without eliciting a strike. The fish, natural skeptics, will sometimes examine a fly carefully without making a decision. At such times a change in the fly's action can stimulate a strike.

The fish are accustomed to seeing emerging insects escape the bottom, drift a short way, and then start on a journey toward the surface. They know the movement. They know too that when the insects start moving upward, they are escaping. The greedy reaction of an undecided fish is to grab before the insect gets away. It's instinctive in all trout.

The fisherman who understands this reaction often can take advantage of the situation. The fly should be fished very carefully in the transition from drift to swing. This is a very high probability spot in the drift. If the fly begins to lift and swing without a jerk or pull, it looks natural and is very enticing to the trout. You can catch lots of fish at this point in the drift.

The problem is that sometimes it's difficult to make a smooth transition. If you've been managing the fly for maximum drift, it may go very suddenly from drift to swing. The transition will be too abrupt; the fly will jerk into a swing rather than flowing into it.

But by mending the proper slack pattern into the line just before the swing starts, you can control the speed of the swing and increase the number of strikes.

There are two approaches. If the belly in the line is large and well formed at the end of the drift, I attempt to lead the fly into the swing. By mending the line down and swinging the rod downstream and ahead of the fly, I can keep the bottom end of the belly curve open. The line forms a half-moon rather than a U shape. Moving the rod off to the side will lead the fly from a drift

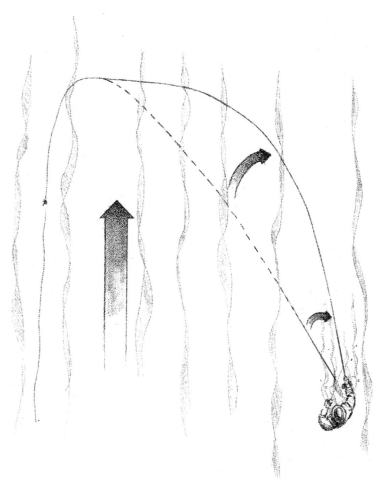

In nymph fishing the transition from drift to swing should be as smooth as possible. The fly should not jerk abruptly into the swing. By mending downstream and leading the fly into the swing with the tip of the rod, the tension and transition can be controlled.

into a swing gradually. Eventually, pressure on the line will sweep the fly away, but the transition from drift to swing will be smooth and attractive to trout.

At other times, when the belly in the line is not so well formed, it may be desirable to make the transition into a controlled swing much like the one used in wet-fly presentation. You would mend the line upstream and reduce the tension by decreasing the size of the belly in the line.

Once you've made the transition, it's important to maintain the swing for a moment. Don't be too quick to cast. Sometimes it takes the fish a moment to get to the fly. The fly in transition from drift to swing has more attractive power than a fly that is just drifting or one that is just swinging. You have to give the fish a chance to cover a greater distance.

Also, there's some delay between the time the indicator begins the transition and the time the fly does. Even with the hinged indicator system, there is some curve in the leader down to the fly. The fly is slightly upstream behind the indicator. The pull on the line has to travel from the indicator to the fly, and the fly doesn't start to swing as soon as the indicator does. You've got to give that fly time to swing for a moment before you move it.

On occasion the lift and swing can be applied as a distinct tactic for reluctant trout. This approach is called the Lisnering lift. In the Lisnering lift, the angler recognizes the value of the transitional stage, so he attempts to make the fly lift directly in front of a sighted trout.

The fly is cast upstream and generally to one side of the fish – slightly toward the angler. It is given enough time to sink to the bottom and begin a dead drift. Then, with a traditional downstream mend, the angler takes slack out of the line to induce the swing to occur just as the fly comes into range of the trout.

Timing of the swing is everything. The fly should lift and swing right under the nose of the reluctant trout. When it's done right, nine times out of ten the fish will instantly respond. The reaction to an escaping fly is so strong that fish have a hard time resisting it.

Transition and swing periods in fishing are very important.

Learning the subtlety of smooth transitions and controlled swings through the proper application of slack can spell the difference between haphazard presentation and a controlled, fish-attracting movement. It's the difference between catching trout and missed opportunities.

12

Controlled Slack
with Streamers
and Sink-Tip Lines

There was a time when I thought streamer fishing was idiot fishing – that it lacked the sophistication and grace of conventional fly tactics. I thought it was a matter of hauling out the big guns, the heavy artillery, the 8-, 9-, and 10-weight rods, and throwing heavy flies and sinking lines as far as you could, and continuing to throw as long as you could until something grabbed.

I've since learned it's more. Through slack and tension control, I've learned to breathe life into my flies. I've learned to make fur and feather swim. But the refinement in streamer fishing came late in the development of my repertoire of fishing skills.

It's odd that many fishermen, like myself, seem to avoid the plunge into streamers.

I knew for a long time that streamers were the way to catch large fish. My home river, the Metolius, has a good population of trophy bull trout, a native species once mistakenly called Dolly Varden. I knew the bull trout were piscivorous—they ate fish. I knew the way to catch them was with streamers. Yet at best I dabbled—I played at fishing with these flies.

Part of the problem is that streamer fishing is specialized fishing. You must make a decision to fish streamers alone; as soon as you haul out the artillery, you are abandoning other trout opportunities.

At the same time, streamer fishing is not fast paced. It deals with the largest fish, the trophy trout, the fish of your dreams. It is obvious that such fish don't come easy.

Streamer fishing requires a commitment to a void. The beginning streamer fisherman must work hard, present well, and not be discouraged by limited results—and we all know that's not easy to do.

Even now, with plenty of years of experience, there are times when I still have to talk to myself saying, "Just because you're not getting results doesn't mean the technique is a failure. Keep working. You'll find the combination; you'll find a fish that's ready."

That kind of commitment is much more difficult if you don't have a history. It's hard to keep fishing if you aren't absolutely convinced that the flies and techniques will work. For the newcomer who hasn't caught many fish with a streamer, it is difficult to persist.

But the techniques are not impossible, and the rewards of streamer fishing are enormous. I know of no other approach that is so consistently effective for trophy-size fish. My personal best, the largest fish I've ever caught in any species, have all come on streamers.

Most streamer fishing is done in the deeper holes where the big fish live; the flies want to be sunk deeply. They want to be fished along the bottom.

There are exceptions, of course. Some streamers can be fished at or near the surface. But it's generally more difficult to draw the fish out than it is to go down to them.

There are two ways to get the fly down. One is to use a long leader, a floating line, and weight in the fly itself; the other is to use sinking or sink-tip lines and a lighter fly. Each method has its advantages.

Whichever method you choose, even with slack presentation, it's going to take more weight than usual to get the fly down. Streamer fishing uses long casts to reach difficult lies. The holes are deep, the drifts are long, and the currents are strong. No matter how good you are at slack line presentation, it will be very difficult to keep all the pull off the line. To compensate for this drag, you have to add weight.

If you choose to use the floating line method, which I prefer, the fly often will need both lead eyes and lead in the body to get to the bottom. If you fish with sinking lines, you will need to use the most extreme sink rates available.

Flies weighted in the extreme tend to be a nightmare to cast. It's the old chuck-and-duck approach – hurl the lead and keep your head down.

Sinking lines, on the other hand, are generally easier to cast, although this can be a matter of preference and of degree. Some of the really heavy sinking lines, the ones that are the most effective in the waters I fish, achieve rapid sink rates by overloading the rod.

Typically a line is balanced to a rod by the number of grains of weight in the first 30 feet of line. The faster-sinking lines achieve their rapid rates in two ways: by concentrating the weight in the tip portion of the line – in 5 feet rather than 30 feet of line – and by overloading the rod by increasing the grains of weight so that a line recommended for a 6- or 7-weight rod would be more properly matched to a 9- or 10-weight rod.

Lines of this type are chunky in the air and hard to cast. They crash forward and back, jerking the rod with each casting stroke.

Nothing I know is going to make large streamers easy to cast. I have experimented extensively in this area. I'm always trying to reduce the weight, but so far these experiments have been relatively unsuccessful.

The question becomes which type of uncomfortable casting you prefer: an overloaded rod crashing back and forth, or an

overweighted fly whistling past your ear as you duck. If you want
to penetrate deeply with large, sunken flies, it's one or the other.
Most casters agree that the lesser of these two evils is the sinking
line. The sinking line, however, has other disadvantages in control that may or may not make it the line of choice.

No matter which method you choose, in all streamer situations there are two general phases of the drift. The first is the
sink, and the second is the swing.

In the sink phase, no matter whether you use sinking lines or
weighted flies, the objective is to get the tension off the line and
allow the fly or line to get down. The roll cast mend is the most
effective tool to accomplish this control. I curl the line around
above the fly with the first cast and then continue to stack-mend
to build an additional slack reserve.

With a sinking line, the initial slack pattern must be set up
very quickly and carefully after the cast. There can be no hesitation. As soon as you stop mending, the weighted line will
sink. Once it is under, there is no further opportunity to make
adjustments.

Even with sink-tip lines, the grip of the water is enough to
severely limit secondary control. Whatever pattern of slack you
have set up in the beginning must be fished through. The sink
phase will lead to the swing; the fly is on its way whether you
like the drift or not.

Once the fly enters the swing, you are attempting to control
slack and at the same time keep a nice, light touch on the fly.
There should be enough tension to be ready if the fish comes, but
the touch should be light enough to avoid pulling the fly too
much, lifting it off the bottom.

The rod follows the fly downriver very much like the control
in a nymph drift, eventually moving ahead to keep the belly out
of the line as long as possible.

The distinction between streamer fishing and nymph fishing
is that with the streamer the fly is fished more actively. It is being
pulled along with a swimming motion as the line forms in a
curve downstream.

By gradually swinging the rod ahead of the fly downstream
the curve of the line can be kept open, a controlled tension is

applied, and the fly is led smoothly across and down. You can add twitches to give an even more lifelike presentation.

I like to think of this style of streamer presentation as being very much like a puppet on a string. The streamer is an imitation of a fish. You want to make it swim. If the imitation looks wounded or injured, it is all the more effective in attracting large predators, as it appears to be a large piece of protein that is easy to catch.

On many rivers in the Northwest there is a run of kokanee, a form of land-locked sockeye salmon. When the kokanee finish their spawn, they die. It's a time for large trout to pack in the calories.

I've stood on the rocks above a deep pool and watched the big heads turn as a half-dead kokanee went through. The kokanee will be drifting, then struggling, then drifting again. The big predator fish are watching. It doesn't take long until one of them will sidle over – and the kokanee is gone.

By playing the tension on the line, by stripping quickly a couple of strokes and then dropping slack, I can imitate the death struggle of a kokanee. I can present a wounded fish struggling to survive. My catch rate goes up enormously.

White flies are wonderful streamers to aid in this type of presentation. White is a color of sickness and injury in a stream. Fungus infections, scars, the belly of a dead or dying fish are all white. When a large predator fish sees white, he sees food. And on the fisherman's part, a white fly is easy to see underwater. If you have reasonably clear conditions in the stream where you're fishing, a white fly can be used as a tool to understand how your fly is behaving. You can watch and learn to make the fly respond – to move it like a puppet on a string. A white fly is the perfect tool to help you understand how to use tension and slack alternately to make the fly appear to be a dead or dying fish.

The white fly is also very useful in searching out new water. Because streamers are fished at long distances on sinking lines, it is often very difficult to know exactly where your fly is and how it is behaving. Under such conditions, I frequently put on a white fly to refine the drift, and then switch to something else later.

It's a tremendous psychological boost to know with absolute

assurance how the motions you're making and the drift you're delivering are affecting the fly. And it's a proven fact that a fly fished with confidence catches more fish.

The puppet-on-a-string, active streamer presentation can be done with either floating or sinking lines, but sinking lines have an advantage because both the line and the fly are down along the bottom. When you twitch or work the fly, the pull is across, not up and away as it is with a floating line.

On the down side, if the riverbottom is obstructed, the sinking line can be a real problem. As it sweeps along, it will find every limb and rock that sticks up, wrap around them, and grab on. You'll quickly be frustrated by the number of lost flies and even more frustrated when you lose a line.

In our area, some of the Oregon coastal streams are examples of good sinking-line water. These freestone rivers have strong floods in the winter rainy season; they tend to flush out. The bottom is covered with rounded boulders, and the fish hang out in depressions in the rocks. The fly and line can be walked along the bottom without a problem.

In contrast, streams like the Metolius, which has an even spring-fed flow, don't get cleaned out. The wood and debris collect, and hazards are everywhere. The fly is better fished from above with a floating line so that it can be maneuvered between the obstacles.

To fish a streamer from a floating line requires more manipulation. You have to mend the line throughout the drift to compensate for the lifting tendency of a system that is fished from the surface down. Both roll cast mends and conventional mends are repeated throughout the swing.

With practice and the help of a white fly to learn the technique, a streamer fisherman can become adept at fishing a fly "puppet" with a dry line.

As a bonus, there are some techniques that work really well with a floating line that cannot be duplicated with sinking or sink-tip lines.

The first of these is hopping. Our friends in the spin and bait fishing world have a popular little lure they call a jig. A jig has a painted lead ball for a head and a colorful feather for a tail. These lures don't imitate anything. The attractive power lies in the motion of the lure when it's activated.

The jig is usually fished out of a boat. The fisherman drops it down to the bottom, then retrieves it with a crank or two and sits lifting and dropping the tip of the rod slowly, waiting for a fish. It's a beer drinker's tactic – boring fishing to me. The value to a fly fisherman is in understanding the motion of the lure.

When pulled, the jig swims upward. When released, it turns over and drops nose-first, swimming downward. It has a swimming motion both vertically and horizontally. The feather swims horizontally, waving with the movement of the lure. The lead head causes the lure to swim vertically.

In the underwater world there are an enormous number of food items that have this vertical-horizontal action. Fish of all types are keyed to it.

In a river, the most common food item with a vertical-horizontal action is the sculpin. The sculpin is a little baitfish common in most rivers. They range up to 3 or 4 inches long, are bulbous in shape, and have no air bladder. They swim and crawl the bottom, eating algae.

Anglers seldom see sculpins because they never come to the surface. But underwater, the fish – especially large predator fish – are very familiar with the sculpin and its behavior.

The sculpins often swim up 6 to 12 inches from the bottom and then drop back with a jig-type action. Underwater, that motion signals a large food item.

To imitate this action, I tie a streamer with lead eyes. I absolutely love these lead-eyed flies for two reasons. First, if the eyes are tied on the top of the hook, they turn the fly over. The lead eyes will be on the bottom and the hook point will be up. I tie the whole fly upside down on the hook. A fly tied in this way can be stopped on the bottom and fished in very close contact to the rocks and logs without hanging up. Second, and even more valuable, the position of the weight at the head functions like the little lead ball on a jig and gives the fly a vertical-horizontal motion.

The hopping technique uses a lead-eyed fly. The fly is cast upstream and then followed with a roll cast mend to provide slack. Once the fly is down, it's allowed to dead-drift the bottom with an occasional twitch. The tension on the fly is carefully controlled so that the twitch will lift the fly off the bottom. The twitch is followed with a drop of the rod tip or possibly even a small roll cast mend to provide slack.

The effect is a fly that will hop the bottom. It lifts and swims 6 to 12 inches upward, then immediately turns over and drops back to the bottom nose-first. It's an exceptionally good imitation of a sculpin traveling downstream and is an irresistible motion to large fish.

An interesting variation on the hop is the controlled stop. The stop technique is not something I'm able to use every day. It requires just the right set of circumstances. It is only effective on sighted fish at fairly close range – not an easy thing to find. When I do come on the right circumstances, however, I've had 80 to 90 percent success with this technique. That's an extremely high success rate – excellent probability. I know of no other technique as consistent, especially for large fish.

The fly is cast upstream of the target and sunk to the bottom. As it comes into range, I throw a very powerful roll cast mend upstream. I want as much extra slack in the line as possible. The

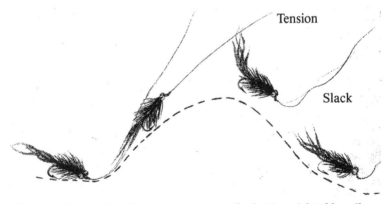

By alternating slack and tension a streamer fly that is weighted heavily in the head can be fished with a swimming motion that is both vertical and horizontal. The fly can be made to hop along the bottom with a very realistic up-and-down motion.

timing of the mend is critical. The objective is to get the fly to stop within a foot or two of the nose of the target fish.

It is not easy to get the stop right. It often takes several attempts to get the fly to do what's wanted. When it does land close enough, however, it's like magic. The fly stops. There's a moment's hesitation. Then it's as if the fish says, "I saw where you went and you're not going to get away from me!" He moves over and vacuums the fly right out of the rocks on the bottom.

I promise you it's an adrenaline junkie's way to catch a fish. Your hands won't stop shaking for an hour after you've watched a 5-pounder gobble your fly that way.

When you get tired of throwing all the weight, another exciting and unusual way to catch a fish on a streamer is wet-fly style, just under the surface. The primary disadvantage of the wet-fly streamer drift is that anytime you use a streamer near the surface, you know you could probably catch more fish if you went down to the bottom. On the plus side, it's a very exciting way to catch a trout.

Wet-fly streamers are best fished early and late in the day. At those times the bigger fish are apt to be more active. Large trout feel more comfortable moving under the cover of low light conditions.

I like to use a very dark fly so that it will be silhouetted plainly against the evening or early morning sky. The fly is fished with a very active presentation.

A fly cast in the traditional way, sunk deep and delivered on the swing, presents itself sideways to the current. It swings and moves across the current lanes, coming down the river broadside through the entire presentation.

But as any fisherman knows, all trout keep their noses up-river into the current. When you fish on top, you have the ability to maneuver the line and fly better, so you can make a more realistic presentation. By using a powerful roll cast mend, I'm able to put an angle in the line and suspend the fly's nose upstream. It's much more lifelike.

I can even add a wrinkle to this presentation called the lane change. When a fish moves from one current lane to the next, it noses over, shows its side to the current, and as soon as the change is made, quickly rights itself. It's a very distinct motion that can be imitated quite precisely with tension followed by a roll cast mend.

With the right mend, I can even throw a loop of slack beyond the fly and make it swim out into the river away from the bank, then let it drift back.

When fished correctly, the presentation looks like a hurt fish, on the surface, struggling to stay upright in the current but with barely enough strength to do it.

The strikes on a wet-fly streamer are spectacular. The predator fish are like sharks. They are not there to swallow a small prey like a little mayfly – they are attacking to kill. They typically strike and injure the prey and then eat it later. The kill blow is like a bomb blast on the river surface. It's a very aggressive

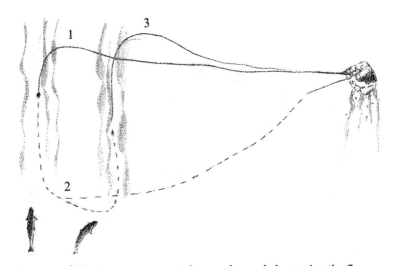

A very realistic streamer presentation can be made by casting the fly cross-stream and following immediately with a roll cast mend. 1. The mend pulls the nose of the streamer upstream. 2. As tension forms on the line the fly will drop away and swim across the current lanes. 3. Mend again to reposition its nose upstream in a position a little closer to the bank. A streamer fished in this way will display behavior closely approximating small bait fish in the river.

attack. The electricity coming down your arm is like plugging into 110 volts.

Streamer fishing is an exciting and wonderful side to the sport of fly fishing. If you've been avoiding it, you should take the time to play the game a bit more. It certainly is rewarding.

The key to good streamer fishing and the reason for slack in streamer techniques is to make the fly look like a fish. Play on the large predator fish's natural instincts – imitate sickness and injury. Show a fly as easy prey; give it a natural, lifelike motion.

You'll find that breathing life into a bit of fur and feather on the end of string is a subtle art. Streamer fishing is not idiot fishing at all – it's a wonderful, little understood side of our magnificent sport.

13

Slack Line Tactics
for Steelhead

Steelhead are almost mystical fish. There are many curious things about them. Their life cycle – that magnificent journey, fighting the odds to battle back upstream to their birthplace so they can spawn in that same gravel – is a wonderful story. We don't really know much about these fish. Despite all the study that's been done, biologists still can't figure out how or why they find their way back home.

The fishermen don't know much either. When they are in the rivers steelhead are not feeding; so why do they react? Why do they take our flies?

Then there's the size of the fish and the power – the size they gain in the ocean, and the power they must have to battle up the rivers.

A fish like that has a way of captivating the imagination. You can't escape the pull. Each season when the steelhead start moving in, there's a sense of expectation in the air.

The stories start circulating well before the main run arrives – an odd fish is caught here and there. Some of it's truth, some is rumor, but you can't help being caught up by it.

When the main run finally does come in, things get crazy. Steelhead fever is on the water. We're up in the frosty morning pulling on frozen boots and waders in the dark. Don't worry about bad weather and the coming winter. Only one thing is on your mind: hour upon hour of fanatical pursuit. Dawn to dark fishing. All for the elusive steelhead.

In our region the most traditional way to fish steelhead is the greased line method. Greased line is an old-fashioned way of saying floating line; it's very much like wet-fly fishing.

The fly is cast across and down and then brought to the fish on the swing. Slack enters the game as a way to control the swing. Conventional mends are made upstream to slow the fly or downstream to accelerate it.

The speed of the swing is critical; a great deal of energy is spent achieving the right "steelhead" motion. The idea is to bring the fly across the steelhead's nose with a slow but steady movement. The tip of the fly line should be curled back slightly so that the fly comes down and across broadside to the current.

Unlike a streamer, which should be fished with the nose of the fly upriver, the steelhead fly should show itself plainly. These flies are attractor patterns that should advertise themselves, but without being gaudy.

A swing that's either too fast or too slow puts fish off. Controlling the swing is an absolutely fundamental part of steelhead technique. Without the ability to control line speed through slack mending, it would be an entirely different sport.

Dry-fly steelheading, or fishing waking patterns, is another area where slack is mended into the line to control the speed of the fly across the water. The steelhead dry fly is not fished dead-drift like a trout fly; instead, it is under tension and a controlled wake is created. The fly should make a V-shaped wake without throwing spray.

The control in this instance is the opposite of that in the

greased line method. By mending downstream to put a controlled belly in the line and at the same time swinging the rod toward the bank at the right speed, tension can be carefully controlled and the fly presented with a soft wake the way steelhead like it.

It requires a touch, but dry-fly steelheading is without question the most exciting way to catch one of these oceangoing trout. The steelhead frequently chase the fly and boil at it several times before they actually strike. Watching one of these big bruisers come to your fly over and over again—waiting for the take—is better than a treadmill for a cardiovascular stress test. You'll sit on the bank for a half hour afterward just to recover.

In steelheading, slack technique is also very useful to control swing at greater distances. Most sophisticated steelheaders believe it is really important to spend a lot of time and energy trying to find fish that are outside the normal lies, fish that may not have been covered by the average angler.

It's well understood in steelheading that the first fly over the fish is usually the best opportunity. The competition to be first is sometimes pretty ugly; it brings out the worst in fishermen. The more creative anglers pull away from the constant battle, the race to be first to the hole, and try to find other, more imaginative, ways to compete.

One way to do this is to cast farther than the other guy—to reach out to steelhead lying beyond the region customarily fished.

The problem with distance casting arises in trying to get control out there. If you cast straight across from your position you get farther out, you gain maximum distance, but as soon as the fly lands, the river begins to force a large belly into the line and the fly will swing too fast. You won't get control of it until it's come to a position quartering downstream where conventional mends can slow the swing. Most steelhead fishermen therefore find no advantage to casting straight across and instead use a quartering downstream approach.

In a situation like this, the roll cast mend can be employed to put an angle in the tip of the line in order to get control of the speed of the fly farther out in the river. The slack line steelheader

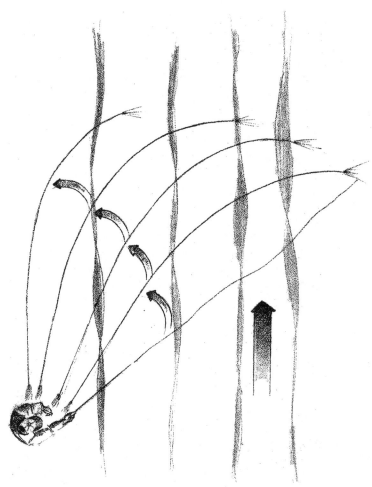

In dry-fly steelheading the wake of the fly is controlled by mending slack out of the line and moving the rod toward the bank to control tension.

casts straight out or slightly down and then follows with a large roll cast mend. He may need to mend several times. Eventually an angle is created in the tip of the line; a swing that achieves steelhead speed can be developed much farther out in the river.

I once had the privilege of watching an old-timer use this technique to blow a young, hotshot steelheader right out of the water. One day, when a friend and I arrived at a popular steelhead run, there were two fishermen there already. A younger fellow was going through first and he was about halfway down the run. An older fellow was just starting in at the top. My partner and I sat on the bank to wait our turn. According to steelhead etiquette, the others would fish through; we'd get a chance in a few minutes.

The young fellow was really belting out some line. He was a good fisherman and was quite strong. He waded deep and cast a long line.

The old fellow behind him was quite frail and seemed to be at an enormous disadvantage—it would have been dangerous for him to wade too deep. He didn't have the power to cast beyond the young man, but he certainly had the technique.

He cast straight out, not quartering down. He got as much distance as his bony, old arm and his extraordinary timing would give him. Then he followed with the roll cast mend, angling the tip of the line. It was fascinating how much farther out in the river he was able to gain control.

I could see the tips of several boulders out there that the young fellow had not covered. They made an excellent steelhead holding lie. The old man obviously knew all about them. It didn't take him long.

We saw the steelhead flash once. "You've got a looker," I called to the old fellow.

"Thanks," he nodded. Two casts later he had the hook up.

I turned to my partner. "I don't think there's much point in going through behind that guy, do you?"

My partner agreed. We went off to look for a run of our own.

Another problem that frequently arises in steelheading is an obstructed backcast. Not all the runs are wide open. Many of the best ones have overhanging alders, high banks, and teasels to

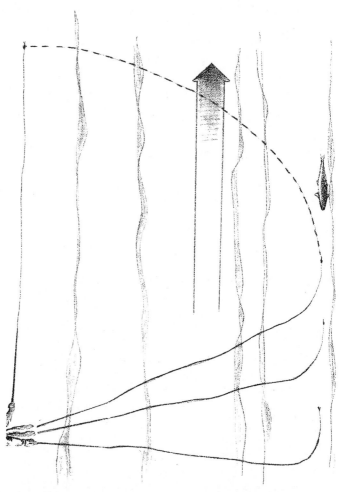

Using the roll cast mend to place slack on an outside current lane will allow a steelheader to start a controlled swing farther out in the river. This technique will help the caster reach more distant, undisturbed steelhead.

contend with. It's roll cast territory. Obviously, in these places it's very advantageous to be able to roll cast more distance.

The distance roll cast starts with a small back stroke not normally employed in a roll cast. The rod tip is up and forward; a loop of line is picked up and thrown to the rear, but it's not thrown overhead. The loop is suspended below the rod tip and goes back about waist-high. The more line you can suspend, the farther you can throw the roll cast in the front.

After the loop is formed in the air, the rod tip is up and slightly back. Before the line settles, you simply make the roll cast stroke – a good, solid stroke with a wrist snap.

The loop thrown in the air behind you will have freed a significant amount of line from the grip of the water. That line is the extra distance you'll be able to cast.

The single disadvantage to the distance roll cast is that unlike a conventional roll cast, it requires a small amount of room behind the caster. The amount of room, however, is far less than would be required to make a similar overhead cast.

To roll cast a greater distance a small loop of slack line must be created in the air behind the caster.

A powerful roll casting stroke will translate the extra slack into extra distance.

A caster who can achieve extra distance roll casting can follow almost anyone else through an obstructed steelhead run and know that he is showing his fly to fresh fish. It won't be long until he starts hooking the fish others could not reach.

Yet another important slack lesson for steelheaders is the parallel between streamer fishing and steelhead fishing. When the water is high, the weather is cold, or for any other reason the steelhead are being sluggish and not moving to the fly, the angler may find it necessary to abandon greased line tactics and go down to the fish.

As soon as you start adding weight to the fly or using weighted lines, you should begin to employ the same tactics described for streamers in chapter 12. You need to mend up to get a better sink rate. You'll want to anticipate the drift and create slack patterns in advance.

The only major difference between streamer and steelhead techniques is that streamers are generally fished more actively than steelhead flies. The streamer is used like a puppet on a string in order to create action that imitates a baitfish. The steelhead seem to prefer a more consistent motion; they like to see a smooth, steady swing. Flies that dart and twitch too actively will spook steelhead rather than attracting them.

Very often that little bit of motion is the only difference between streamer and steelhead fishing. Even the flies are becoming more similar; ever increasingly, small streamers like the Woolly Bugger, Bunny Leech, and Slink Leech are being employed successfully to catch both steelhead and trout.

The most recent addition to the slack line steelheader's arsenal of tactics is dead-drifted flies. As nymphing skills have improved, more and more steelhead fishermen are discovering how well a fly with no motion at all attracts steelhead.

The hinged indicator system has played a pivotal role in this steelhead revolution. Hickson and Schubert, the inventors of the system, first developed the idea for trout but soon began to use the hinged indicator for steelhead on the North Umpqua River.

The Umpqua has long been world renowned as a haven for both steelhead and fly fishermen. The river is deep, swift, and clear. The steelheaders often get up on high banks above the holes and spot fish with binoculars, then try to fish them out. Commonly two anglers work together, one spotting and one fishing.

Sometimes with a traditional approach it is easy to spot the fish and hard to make them move. Hickson and Schubert began to employ the indicator method on these stubborn, reluctant fish. Their tactics were very much like trout tactics. The only significant difference was that they used heavier line and flies to accommodate the extra strength and power of the fish they were after.

A number of different flies can be used to attract steelhead with dead-drift tactics. Sometimes weighted flies are used; stonefly nymphs and variations, such as the Girdle Bug, are most common. At other times very small nymphs like Pheasant Tails and Hare's Ears are used with a split shot on the line. Why the big fish go for such little flies is a mystery to us all, but it does work. In recent years, while employing dead-drifted nymph tactics for steelhead, my clients and I have repeatedly caught fish on flies as small as #14, #16, and once even a little bitsy #18. What a wrestling match trying to land a 5-pound steelhead on a #18 fly!

Apparently the fish remember the small nymphs from their days as little steelhead smolts growing up in the river. They pick them up either as a reflex action or out of curiosity, to see if they still taste good.

A third category of flies that work well with dead-drift tactics are the egg patterns—the Glo Bugs and Sparkle Eggs. The single egg has long been the steelhead drift fisherman's favorite weapon. Spin and bait fishermen use heavy lead weights attached to the line and bounce the bottom dead-drift with single egg patterns, both real and artificial.

The two-tone yellow and orange plastic strike indicators that we fly fishermen commonly put on the line with a toothpick are actually steelhead lures called corkies. Lure fishermen sometimes use a corky like a single egg without flashers or any other attractions. It's very effective for steelhead.

Knowing this, fly fishermen in recent years have adapted the hinged indicator system to duplicate the look of the drift-fishing presentation. They tie on single egg flies and dead-drift them on the bottom, matching the speed of the current just like a nymph-fishing presentation.

Dead-drift steelhead tactics work best to specific locations: to a sighted steelhead or to a drift that is known. For example, if there is a slot where steelhead lie or a specific boulder where they always hang out, a nymphing approach will generally allow the angler to cover that water more thoroughly.

The nymphing approach is also better in the daylight. The fly goes down to the bottom right to the fish. It is most effective on fish that aren't moving—fish that need to see a fly presented right on the nose.

The traditional method, on the other hand, is better for covering broad steelhead riffles with less-defined cover. It will search a large area more thoroughly. It's better, too, in the early morning and late evening when fish are more active—when the steelhead are more willing to move to the fly.

The dead-drift techniques, when applied properly, have proven to be so deadly that they've stirred enormous controversy.

On the Umpqua, two schools of thought have formed: Arguments between the traditionalists and the nymphing steelheaders have spilled over into the popular press.

The traditionalists believe that the old ways should be preserved. They contend that indicator fishing for steelhead is outside the bounds of tradition and should not be accepted as a fly-fishing tactic.

The problems they see with nymphing tactics are multifold. First, the fact that single eggs and dead-drifted nymphs can move otherwise dour steelhead means that some of the fish never become fresh enough to move to swinging surface patterns. They are stung over and over again down deep and never get a chance to recover.

Second, the traditionalists claim, slack line nymph-fishing methods injure a lot of fish without ever hooking them. They point out, correctly, that at times in order to get the drift, the nymph-fishing steelheader uses so much slack he loses control. Fish may be nicked but not hooked solidly. This concern may sound a little odd coming from someone who would like to hook the fish himself, but on the Umpqua the fish are like demigods. One should not mess with the spirits of the river in a frivolous way. Hook 'em or leave 'em is the sentiment.

Perhaps worse than either of these criticisms is the fact that the traditional and nymphing steelheaders have very different approaches to the water. The traditionalist generally starts at the top of the run, casting and moving down one or two steps with each presentation. This method of casting and moving promotes the orderly progression of fishermen through the water.

If you come on a piece that's being fished, you simply wait your turn to start at the top following through; in that way each fisherman has an opportunity at the run and at the prime lies within the run. No one stays on any one piece of water too long.

The nymphers, on the other hand, don't move as much. They tend to spot a fish and present repeatedly until they get a take. The lack of orderly movement disrupts the traditional step-down cycle.

The nymph-fishing steelheaders are quick to counter these arguments with ideas of their own. They say complaints that nymphers hook too many fish are nothing but sour grapes. Fishing is and always has been first-come, first-served. If one fisherman can get to the steelhead first by going down deep before another can get them on top, good for him. He just outfished the guy who won't adapt. The nymphers think the traditionalists just don't like being outfished.

The nymphing steelheaders go on to say that there's no real movement conflict, because the two groups tend to fish at different times of the day. The nymphers like midday when the sun is on the water and fish are easiest to spot. The traditionalists like to fish in the early morning or late evening when the light is off the water and the fish are more active. A nympher usually doesn't appear on the water until ten o'clock. At that point, the traditionalist has been out since sunup and he's getting ready to go back for a nap. So there shouldn't be any conflict at all.

But when the two do meet on the water, the nymphers say they are just as aware of other fishermen as anybody else. They claim to know and abide by the unspoken etiquette.

The nymphers answer the accusation that they don't share the water by saying that it's not a problem with the method, it's a problem with the individual anglers. There are rude fishermen who don't share the water in both camps. The method has nothing to do with manners.

In my opinion, each side of the discussion has some merit. I see a real danger in traditional thinking blocking the path to new ideas. The arguments against nymphing steelhead remind me of the old Halford-Skues arguments, with Halford the dry-fly man saying Skues the upstart nympher was a heretic. Today those arguments seem pretty silly.

In any definition of fly fishing, there has to be room to explore and to discover new ways of doing things. For me new knowledge is the heart and soul of fly fishing. When there is nothing new to learn and no new challenge, I will move on to another sport. I strongly resent efforts to limit the way I engage in my sport. I feel it's important to stretch the bounds of our knowledge.

But in defense of traditional thinking, I don't want to lose the old way of doing things, either. I find a very special enjoyment in fishing a steelhead fly on the swing. I take pleasure in the history of our sport. It's wonderful to be on a river like the Umpqua and think of all the famous fishermen who have gone through that same water ahead of you. It's like being a part of living history.

Each technique has its own merit. Each has a time and place where it is most effective.

The nymph-fishing steelheader should not be too quick to say that all the traditional arguments are sour grapes or to brag about how well the new methods work. Most of all, he must consider how his actions affect other fishermen. The new kid on the block always has something to show the old-timer. He must also show, however, that he can fit in without conflict. I don't think that goal is impossible to achieve. I hope that in the long run fishermen will come to understand that there is no one right way to do things and that we all have to work to get along with one another.

I sincerely wish that we fly fishermen could stop bickering with one another over method and begin to work together on the real issues. The big problem on trout and steelhead streams everywhere in the world is diminishing natural resources. We're losing clean water, natural habitat, and the genes of the native fish at an alarming rate.

Our energies should be directed at preserving these natural resources. If we don't do so, the arguments over technique could be moot – there might not be any steelhead left to fish for.

14

The Final Goal:
The Casting Dance

Each slack line caster has his own style. The way an individual
fishes is as personal as a fingerprint. If you spend some time with
a good slack liner, you'll soon be able to recognize him by his
style a mile off down the river.

David Soares has a tight look. He masks his slack line ability.
His casting is understated, and his movements are subdued. It's a
clean, efficient style.

David Renton is more flamboyant. Sometimes he looks like
he's conducting an orchestra. He has a dynamic, gesturing rod
movement that rolls out the slack.

Bob Newton is always pointed downriver. His rod tip jumps
repeatedly as he feeds out slack using the flip method.

For any fishing problem, there's likely to be more than one

solution. Each slack line caster will choose a solution according to his own ability and experience.

Bob Newton likes downstream casting because he's had luck with it; it works well where he fishes. When Bob is faced with a problem, he'll seek a downstream solution.

David Renton is an indicator man. He'll stack mend and roll cast mend to find his solution. His rod has the larger motion of a water-casting fisherman.

David Soares is a dry-fly man. He loves small dries. If he can, he'll find a solution using the upstream approach, with bounce and S casts.

Each of these men is capable of using more than one approach. They can alter their style. David Soares will fish down when the conditions require it, and Bob Newton will fish up. But given a choice, they'll go back to their own signature style. Over time and experience, they've found what they prefer—what they're most comfortable with. That has become their style, and without thinking they move toward it.

Developing a personal style should be the goal for every slack liner. Early in the learning process, when faced with a problem, we all tend to concentrate on technique. Eventually, though, slack and the solutions to problems should become second nature; the fisherman should be able to use various techniques to solve most problems without having to think about it first.

I don't move down the river thinking about every cast. I'm not saying to myself. "What's the problem here? How do I attack this?" Usually I look and I know automatically what to do.

Once slack line has become second nature, you begin to develop a style—you'll have a new freedom of movement, and the rod will almost seem to have a life of its own. There is a marvelous beauty and grace in the way the line unfolds, the slack rolls out, and everything begins to flow with the river. It's almost like a dance.

A technique is no longer steps A, B, C, and D; it is a movement as a whole. You don't think—you do.

As I started doing the research for this book, I consulted with many friends and acquaintances about various aspects of slack line strategy. We would go out in the yard and try to puzzle out what it is we do and how we do it. We all were casting experts, yet many of us had never tried to articulate what we know—to break it down, thinking about it step by step, and to describe it. We thought of these techniques, these movements, as a whole and not as parts.

When your casting begins to dance, the lines between techniques become blurry. We had to spend quite a bit of time thinking, talking, and discussing to determine the parts of some of the techniques.

For example, sometimes it can be difficult to separate a positive curve cast from a reach. The positive curve is an over-powered side-arm bounce cast. When you lock your muscles to make the rod snap, your hand automatically bounces back slightly. As you become used to the casting technique, this bounce back or recoil leads almost instinctively into a reach cast. There will almost always be some element of a reach at the end of a positive curve cast. Where does one begin and the other end? Who knows and who really cares? What's important is that the rod responds and the slack pattern that counterbalances the river current is created.

The beginning caster lays the line on the water first, then mends to create a slack pattern. The advanced caster knows that one step follows the other; he may begin to throw mends even before the line has touched the water.

Once the cast is made, the rod is free to move wherever the caster deems it necessary. He performs a complex reach that is really a mend done before the line touches the water. Is it a reach or a mend? It doesn't really matter what you call it; it is a response to the river—a solution to a problem made even before the problem is consciously recognized. The line and fly land on the water fishing.

The casting "dancer" gives no thought to where one technique begins and the other leaves off. There are only problems and solutions and casts in the air.

Of course, reaching this final goal, learning to do this casting dance—to perform instinctively—is not something that comes to a fisherman overnight. It takes time and practice.

The place to start is with good, basic casting fundamentals. Learn the basic techniques of loop control and rod snap. I know of no good slack liner who is not also a sound fundamental caster.

You don't necessarily have to be a distance caster; you don't need to be the guy who can win all the contests. But you should be a sound caster – one who will deport himself well in any group of fishermen.

Once you have a sound basic casting technique, you can begin to go beyond the limits of straight overhead casting and develop a style of your own. Flexibility will come into your rod movement, and you'll become creative with your casting. Eventually you'll achieve freedom of movement. The rod becomes an extension of your arm. The slack dances in the air. Casting is elevated to an art form that is more than just a way to get the job done; it's a pleasure of its own.

Not long ago a friend was complaining to me about the fishing. It was a spring day and the rivers were high and blown out. There wasn't much going on, and he had suffered a series of unsuccessful outings. "But I had some fun playing with the indicator," he admitted. "I was trying it on different currents just to see if I could get it to work."

He did not need the fish. He had found pleasure in the casting art form. He'd had fun solving the problems even when there were no fish there to make the final judgment of his success.

Developing skill as a slack liner has a pleasure all its own. It is something to enjoy whatever your level. And it is something that will never be finished: No matter how good you get, there is still room to grow.

My technique is continually evolving and changing shape. It will never have a final form. I go through periods, just like a painter. One year is devoted to streamers, the next to indicators and nymphs. The year after that may be dry flies. It's hard to say. New observations and new understanding bring on new problems and new solutions.

As soon as I get some mastery of a technique and start to catch fish with it, I find myself unavoidably moving on to the next problem, the next solution, the next casting technique, the next tool to get the job done. I find I enjoy the problem solving and skill development almost as much as the actual trout on the line. New challenges draw me – I cannot resist them.

This is the essence of slack line: It is the art of getting a drift and catching a fish where no one else can.

Part of the game is being persistent. Slack line skill does not come easy. You must train yourself. Often it is discouraging. I'll admit there have been times when I was ready to quit – times when I got so frustrated I couldn't understand why I would continue. It is, after all, a sport; it's supposed to be fun. Why blow a blood vessel?

But even when it's discouraging, you cannot give up. You must be persistent, continuing to work and chip away until you find solutions. And you must learn to be creative. The slack liner must become an inventor and create solutions to problems. He must not be afraid to experiment.

Those looking for pat answers and fixed solutions probably will not be interested in slack. Nothing is fixed; the problems and the solutions are as individual as the rivers.

Experimenting is how we find the bounds, the limits of our tools and techniques. We must discover what can be done with a fly rod and reel and line. In the end, slack line is all about becoming a better fisherman. It is the way to achieve better and better results in an increasingly complex fly-fishing world.

There was a day when you could walk up to a stream and throw out almost any fly and catch a fish. Those were the "good old days" that Grandpa knew. But those days are gone.

Even with the marvelous strides we've made with catch and release, with trout populations on many rivers restored to near historic levels, fishing still isn't like it was in Grandpa's day. An increasing human population has made the fishing world increasingly complex. It demands more from us as anglers than ever before.

We must become more and more skilled in the way we choose and present our flies. We must find more and more creative solutions for the problems the rivers bring. In short, we must become good slack line fishermen.

I hope that you'll be able to incorporate the ideas presented in this book into your own fishing and that you'll develop your own style for your own river. A greater understanding of slack line strategies should help you to become a better fisherman.

Index